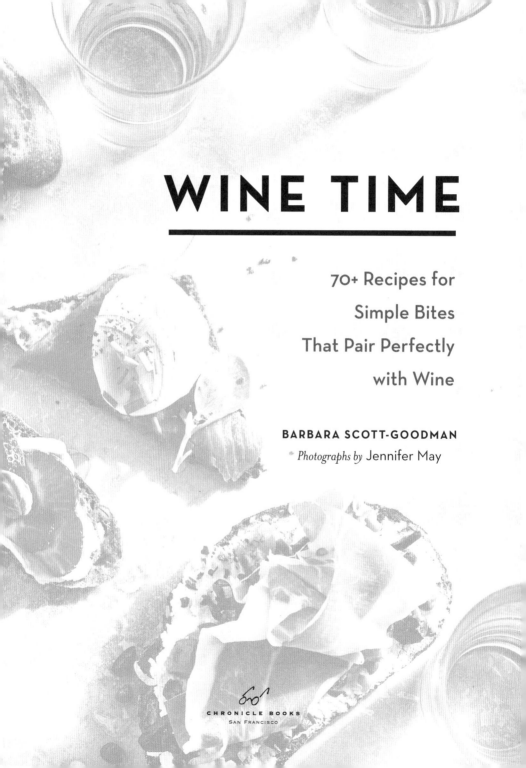

WINE TIME

70+ Recipes for
Simple Bites
That Pair Perfectly
with Wine

BARBARA SCOTT-GOODMAN

Photographs by Jennifer May

CHRONICLE BOOKS
SAN FRANCISCO

Library of Congress Cataloging-in-Publication Data

Names: Scott-Goodman, Barbara, author. | May, Jennifer, photographer.
Title: Wine time : 70+ recipes for simple bites that pair perfectly with wine /
   Barbara Scott-Goodman ; photography by Jennifer May.
Description: San Francisco : Chronicle Books, 2021. | Includes index. |
Identifiers: LCCN 2020019823 | ISBN 9781452181868 (hardcover) |
   ISBN 9781452181882 (ebook)
Subjects: LCSH: Cooking. | Food and wine pairing. | Wine and wine making. |
   LCGFT: Cookbooks.
Classification: LCC TX714 .S3925 2020 | DDC 641.5--dc23
   LC record available at https://lccn.loc.gov/2020019823

Manufactured in China.

Design by Barbara Scott-Goodman and Vanessa Dina.

Food styling by Cyd Raftus McDowell and Cindi Gasparre.

Aperol and Aperol Spritz are registered trademarks of Davide Campari - Milano S.P.A.;
Campari is a registered trademark of Davide Campari - Milano S.P.A.; Clover Club is a
registered trademark of Loew's Hotels, Inc.; Coach Farm is a registered trademark of
Coach Farm Enterprises, Inc.; Cocchi is a registered trademark of Giulio Cocchi Spumanti
S.R.L.; Cypress Grove Chevre is a registered trademark of Cypress Grove Chevre, Inc.;
Goat Lady Dairy is a registered trademark of Tate Family Farm, Inc.; Grand Marnier is a
registered trademark of Marnier-Lapostolle Bisquit Société Anonyme; Laura Chenel is a
registered trademark of Laura Chenel's Chevre, Inc.; St-Germain is a registered trademark
of Bacardi & Company Limited Corporation; Vermont Creamery is a registered trademark
of Vermont Butter and Cheese Creamery, Inc.

10 9 8 7 6 5 4 3 2 1

Chronicle books and gifts are available at special quantity discounts to
corporations, professional associations, literacy programs, and other
organizations. For details and discount information, please contact our
premiums department at corporatesales@chroniclebooks.com or at
1-800-759-0190.

Chronicle Books LLC
680 Second Street
San Francisco, California 94107
www.chroniclebooks.com

For my family and friends,
with whom I've had so many wonderful times
at tables full of good food, wine, and cheer.

CONTENTS

INTRODUCTION

My idea of a good party is to gather a group of friends and enjoy some great
food and wine together. Either for a casual evening or a big-deal cocktail party,
I know that my guests will want something delicious to eat while they're sipping
and chatting. This may sound easier said than done, but *Wine Time* is here
to help.

This book is a collection of recipes and ideas for preparing delectable treats
for all kinds of get-togethers, from small, low-key affairs to big, festive bashes,
and everything else in between. This is food that is fun to make, eat, and enjoy.
Whether you're preparing bite-size snacks to nibble on, savory seafood or
meat dishes to pair with a good bottle, or sumptuous platters of cheese and
charcuterie, this book includes a number of dishes that will fit the bill for any
type of gathering and complement all styles of wine.

A word here about wine: Almost all food goes well with wine. Even though
there are so-called rules about pairing certain wines with certain foods, feel
free to throw these out the window. What matters most is that you enjoy the
wine you buy and drink. I recommend that you let your palate be your guide:
Use my pairing suggestions as starting points, and then try a lot of different
wines with various foods until you figure out what you like.

When shopping for wine, take full advantage of your wine merchant's expertise. Most people are in the wine game because they are passionate about it and they enjoy recommending wines. They're willing to help you find the right wine for every occasion. The same goes for local farmers, butchers, fishmongers, cheesemongers, and gourmet shopkeepers. In my experience, they love to share their opinions, ideas, and knowledge about food, cooking, and ingredients, and I always take their advice to heart.

There is nothing better than the simple pleasure of eating good food and drinking wine with family and friends. But let's be honest: How pleasant is a plate of bread, cheese, and olives with a nice glass of red and a good book in hand? What a way to pass some quality alone time. Whether gathering a crowd or treating yourself, good food and a great glass of wine raise our spirits and enhance our lives, and *Wine Time* will make them even more festive, fun, and memorable.

OK, let's celebrate!

CHAPTER 1

SNACKS & BITES

When your guests arrive, offer them a few simple but tasty snacks to nibble on while you get drinks together. Zesty finger foods, such as spicy nuts, marinated olives with feta cheese, and deviled eggs, can all be eaten in one or two delectable bites, with or without a wineglass in hand.

PARMESAN ROASTED CHICKPEAS

SERVES 8 TO 10

Two 15½ oz [445 g] cans
chickpeas, rinsed
and drained

½ cup [15 g] freshly grated
Parmesan cheese

3 Tbsp extra-virgin olive oil

1 tsp minced garlic

½ tsp paprika

Pinch of cayenne pepper

Kosher salt and freshly
ground black pepper

It's amazing how handy a few cans of chickpeas in the pantry can be. You can use them to make hummus or top salads, rice, and grains; plus, these versatile legumes make a great savory snack when roasted with olive oil, garlic, and a coating of Parmesan cheese. They pair well with a red Merlot or a white Chardonnay.

Arrange the chickpeas on a baking sheet lined with paper towels and let them dry for about 30 minutes. Transfer to a large bowl.

Preheat the oven to 400°F [200°C].

In a medium bowl, stir together the Parmesan, 1½ tablespoons of the oil, the garlic, paprika, and cayenne until well mixed. Pour over the chickpeas and toss well to coat.

Spread the chickpeas in a single layer on a rimmed baking sheet, drizzle with the remaining 1½ tablespoons of oil, and season with salt and pepper. Bake for 20 minutes, stir, and continue to bake until the chickpeas are crisp and golden, about 5 minutes more.

Remove from the oven and transfer to paper towels to drain. Let cool completely. Taste and adjust the seasoning, if necessary, and serve.

MAKE AHEAD: The chickpeas can be made up to 4 hours in advance and can be stored in an airtight container at room temperature for up to 1 day.

SPICY GLAZED CASHEWS

SERVES 6 TO 8

2 cups [280 g] raw unsalted cashews

1½ Tbsp honey

1 Tbsp balsamic vinegar

2 Tbsp extra-virgin olive oil

1 tsp finely chopped fresh thyme

Pinch of cayenne pepper

Kosher salt and freshly ground black pepper

1 Tbsp sesame seeds

1 tsp fresh lemon juice

Here is an easy recipe that combines cashews with olive oil, vinegar, honey, and a hint of cayenne pepper. It's a perfect crunchy cocktail snack. These nuts taste great with a glass of rosé or a light, fruity red such as Pinot Noir or Grenache.

Place the cashews in a medium bowl. In a small bowl, whisk together the honey and vinegar and pour over the nuts. Toss until the nuts are completely coated.

In a large skillet, heat the oil over medium heat. Add the nuts and cook, stirring constantly, until they are golden brown and glazed, about 5 minutes. Be careful not to burn them. Add the thyme and cayenne, season with salt and pepper, and stir.

Remove the pan from the heat. Sprinkle the nuts with the sesame seeds and lemon juice and stir. Spread the nuts out on a baking sheet and let cool for 1 to 2 hours before serving.

MAKE AHEAD: The nuts will keep, covered in an airtight container, for up to 3 days.

CANDIED WALNUTS & PECANS

SERVES 6 TO 8

⅓ cup [65 g] granulated sugar

2 Tbsp brown sugar

1 tsp ground cinnamon

½ tsp kosher salt

¼ tsp cayenne pepper

1 large egg white, at room temperature

1 cup [120 g] whole walnuts

1 cup [120 g] whole pecans

This flavorful mix of nuts is slow-roasted in the oven with a salty, sweet, and spicy coating. Be sure to roast them on sheets of parchment paper since they can be quite sticky when they come out of the oven. Serve these with a light, citrusy Albariño or a buttery Chardonnay.

Preheat the oven to 300°F [150°C]. Line a rimmed baking sheet with parchment paper.

In a small bowl, mix together the granulated and brown sugars, cinnamon, salt, and cayenne.

In a large bowl, whisk the egg white until frothy; add 1 tablespoon of water and whisk until combined. Add the walnuts and pecans and stir to coat. Sprinkle the sugar mixture over the nuts and stir to coat evenly.

Spread the nuts in a single layer on the prepared baking sheet. Bake for 15 minutes, stir the nuts, and continue baking until the nuts are toasted and the sugar coating is caramelized, another 12 to 15 minutes.

Let the nuts cool on the pan, separating them as they cool.

MAKE AHEAD: The nuts will keep, covered in an airtight container, for up to 1 week. Keep in mind that the flavor will become hotter the longer they are stored.

ORANGE-SCENTED OLIVES & FETA CHEESE

SERVES 6

1 cup [140 g] pitted black olives, such as kalamata, drained

3 garlic cloves, peeled and smashed

½ cup [120 ml] extra-virgin olive oil

1 Tbsp fresh orange juice

1 Tbsp orange zest

1 tsp chopped fresh rosemary, plus more for garnish

½ tsp red pepper flakes

8 oz [230 g] feta cheese, preferably French, at room temperature

Freshly ground black pepper

Warm pita bread, cut into triangles, for serving

The combination of black olives, oranges, and tangy feta cheese is fantastic, and this quick and easy dish is one that you will want to serve often. Look for mild and creamy French feta cheese—it plays beautifully with the salty flavor of the olives—and serve with warm pita triangles. To match the saltiness of the feta and olives, drink a bright red wine such as Beaujolais or a light white Greek wine like Assyrtiko with this.

Place the olives, garlic, olive oil, orange juice, orange zest, rosemary, and red pepper flakes in a medium saucepan and cook over medium-low heat, stirring occasionally, until the garlic is sizzling and golden, about 10 minutes.

Crumble the feta into a shallow bowl or plate. Remove and discard the garlic from the pan, pour the olive mixture over the cheese, and let marinate for about 30 minutes. Sprinkle with black pepper and rosemary and serve at room temperature with warm pita triangles. This dish doesn't keep well and is best enjoyed the day it's made.

DEVILED EGGS
WITH SMOKED PAPRIKA BREAD CRUMBS

MAKES 12 DEVILED EGGS

EGGS:
6 large eggs

FILLING:
½ cup [120 g] mayonnaise

1 tsp Dijon mustard

Pinch of dry mustard

Pinch of superfine sugar

Kosher salt and freshly
ground black pepper

Creamy, delicious deviled eggs are usually the first things to disappear from the table at parties and picnics. There are so many ways to prepare them, and in this version, they are topped with toasted fresh bread crumbs and sweet smoked paprika just before serving. This recipe is adapted from the kitchen at Clover Club, a very stylish cocktail bar in Brooklyn, New York, where craft cocktails and fabulous food are on the menu. These taste great with a Cabernet Franc as well as a dry martini.

To make the eggs: Place the eggs in a single layer in a large pot and add cold water to cover the eggs by 1 inch [2.5 cm]. Bring to a gentle boil over medium-high heat. Remove from the heat and cover tightly. Let the eggs stand, covered, for 10 minutes.

Drain and rinse the eggs under cold water. Pat the eggs dry and let cool completely.

Carefully peel the eggs and cut them in half lengthwise. Gently scoop the yolks into a medium bowl, being careful not to break the whites. Arrange the egg whites, cavity-side up, on a platter and set aside.

To make the filling: Mash the yolks with a fork. Add the mayonnaise, mustards, and sugar. Season with salt and pepper and mix until smooth.

Using a small spoon or a piping bag, mound the filling into the cavities of the egg white halves.

TOPPING:

8 slices white bread, crusts removed

2 Tbsp extra-virgin olive oil

1 Tbsp unsalted butter

1 garlic clove, minced

2 tsp sweet smoked paprika, plus more for garnish

Kosher salt and freshly ground black pepper

To make the topping: Preheat the oven to 350°F [180°C].

Place the bread in a food processor and pulse into fine crumbs.

Heat the oil and butter in a large skillet over medium heat until the butter is melted. Add the garlic and cook for 1 minute. Add the bread crumbs and stir until coated.

Spread the bread crumbs onto a baking sheet and bake, stirring occasionally, until golden brown, 5 to 7 minutes. Remove from the oven, sprinkle with the paprika, and season with salt and pepper, tossing well.

Top each deviled egg with a generous spoonful of the bread crumb mixture, sprinkle with a bit more smoked paprika, if desired, and serve.

MAKE AHEAD: The deviled eggs, without the topping, can be refrigerated for up to 3 hours. Top with the bread crumbs and paprika just before serving.

DEVILED EGGS WITH CAVIAR & DILL

MAKES 12 DEVILED EGGS

EGGS:
6 large eggs

FILLING:
½ cup [120 g] mayonnaise

¼ cup [10 g] chopped fresh flat-leaf parsley

1 tsp Dijon mustard

½ tsp white wine vinegar

Kosher salt and freshly ground black pepper

TOPPING:
¾ cup [180 g] sour cream

¼ cup [55 g] salmon caviar

Chopped fresh dill, for garnish

Here is an elegant way to serve this classic snack featuring beautiful, plump, orange pearls of salmon caviar as a topping. Serve with Champagne, Cava, or sparkling wine.

To make the eggs: Prepare the eggs as directed on page 18.

To make the filling: Mash the yolks with a fork. Add the mayonnaise, parsley, mustard, and vinegar. Season with salt and pepper and mix until smooth.

Using a small spoon or a piping bag, mound the filling into the cavities of the egg white halves.

To make the topping: Spoon 1 tablespoon of the sour cream and ½ teaspoon of caviar over each egg half. Garnish the eggs with dill and serve.

MAKE AHEAD: The deviled eggs, without the topping, can be refrigerated for up to 3 hours. Top with sour cream, caviar, and dill just before serving.

MORE DEVILED EGG IDEAS

There are so many delicious ways to make deviled eggs. Here are a few variations to try, which add some new ingredients to the standard egg filling (page 18) and an array of tasty garnishes.

* Add 2 tsp sweet pickle relish and 1 tsp sriracha. Garnish with chopped fresh flat-leaf parsley.

* Add 2 Tbsp each finely chopped red onions and drained capers, plus a pinch of cayenne pepper. Garnish with a red bell pepper strip.

* Add ¼ cup [55 g] finely chopped smoked salmon, 2 Tbsp finely minced fresh dill, and fresh lemon juice to taste. Garnish with a dill sprig.

* Add ¼ cup [55 g] finely chopped crabmeat and fresh lemon juice to taste. Garnish with minced chives.

* Add 2 Tbsp each finely chopped ham and watercress. Garnish with a watercress sprig.

* Add 2 Tbsp each horseradish and finely chopped fresh flat-leaf parsley. Garnish with crumbled bacon.

PICKLED EGGS

MAKES 24 PICKLED EGGS

12 large eggs

2 cups [480 ml] distilled white vinegar

2 small beets, peeled and thinly sliced

¼ cup [40 g] kosher salt

¼ cup [50 g] sugar

1 tsp whole black peppercorns

1 tsp allspice berries

1 tsp juniper berries

1 tsp coriander seeds

2 bay leaves

Extra-virgin olive oil, for serving

Sea salt and freshly ground black pepper, for serving

Pickled eggs are often served at bars and pubs as a good snack to nosh on with a beer. In this version, hard-boiled eggs are steeped in spicy brine and slices of fresh beets that turn the eggs a gorgeous shade of fuchsia. For a hearty and satisfying appetizer, serve them with an assortment of smoked meats, sausages, and black bread. Although beer is often considered the perfect beverage to accompany pickled foods, Riesling and Muscadet go very well with them too.

Place the eggs in a single layer in a large pot and add cold water to cover the eggs by 1 inch [2.5 cm]. Bring to a gentle boil over medium-high heat. Remove from the heat and cover tightly. Let the eggs stand, covered, for 10 minutes. Drain and rinse the eggs under cold water. Pat the eggs dry and let cool completely. When cool, peel the eggs and set aside.

In a large saucepan, combine the vinegar, beets, 1 cup [240 ml] of water, the salt, sugar, pepper-corns, allspice berries, juniper berries, coriander seeds, and bay leaves and bring to a boil over high heat, stirring to dissolve the salt and sugar.

Divide the pickling liquid and beets into two clean 2 quart [2 L] jars with lids. Add 6 eggs to each jar, making sure that they are completely covered. Gently tap the jar a few times to remove any air bubbles. Cover tightly and let cool to room temperature.

Cut the eggs in half lengthwise, drizzle with olive oil, sprinkle with sea salt and pepper, and serve.

MAKE AHEAD: Refrigerate the eggs for up to 1 week before serving.

MUSHROOM & GOAT CHEESE PHYLLO BITES

SERVES 6 TO 8

1 lb [455 g] cremini
  mushrooms

1 Tbsp extra-virgin olive oil

1½ Tbsp butter

3 large green onions (white
  and green parts), trimmed
  and minced

1 Tbsp chopped fresh
  thyme

Kosher salt and freshly
  black ground pepper

⅓ cup [70 g] goat cheese,
  at room temperature

24 frozen mini phyllo cups
  (see Note)

These rich and delicious little cups are filled with a mixture of herbed cremini mushrooms and creamy goat cheese and pair very well with a full-bodied white wine like Pinot Gris or a fruit-forward Pinot Noir.

Trim the stem ends from the mushrooms and wipe the caps clean with a damp paper towel. Cut them into halves or quarters, depending on their size. Put half of the mushrooms in a food processor and pulse until just coarsely chopped. Transfer to a bowl and repeat with the remaining mushrooms.

Heat the olive oil and 1 tablespoon of the butter in a large sauté pan over medium heat until the butter is foaming but not brown. Stir in the green onions and cook until wilted, about 1 minute. Sprinkle the thyme over the green onions and stir for a few seconds. Add the mushrooms, season with salt and pepper, and stir constantly until the mushrooms begin to change color. Cook, stirring occasionally, until the mushrooms give up a lot of liquid. Increase the heat to medium-high and continue cooking until all of the liquid evaporates and the mushrooms start to sizzle in the fat. Cook and stir until the mushrooms are well browned, about 5 minutes.

Scrape the mushrooms into a bowl. Stir in the remaining 1/2 tablespoon of butter and let cool. Stir in the goat cheese.

Preheat the oven to 375°F [190°C]. Place the frozen phyllo cups on a baking sheet. Fill the cups with the mushroom mixture, mounding it slightly. Bake until the cups are crisp and the mushroom mixture is lightly browned, 15 to 18 minutes. Serve warm.

NOTE: Mini phyllo cups are available in the freezer section of supermarkets and online. Do not thaw them before baking. This dish doesn't keep well and is best enjoyed the day it's made.

FIGS WITH SERRANO HAM & BASIL

SERVES 6 TO 8

12 small ripe figs, halved

1 tsp sherry vinegar

½ tsp sugar

¼ tsp ground cumin

4 oz [115 g] thinly sliced
   Serrano ham

24 small basil leaves

Every cook should have a few easy, no-cooking-required hors d'oeuvre recipes for warm-weather parties. This is a terrific one. It requires little more than fresh figs, Serrano ham, and fresh basil leaves. You can also substitute other fruits, such as peaches, nectarines, or plums, for the figs. These sweet and salty bites always taste wonderful with Prosecco or Chianti.

In a large bowl, toss the figs with the vinegar, sugar, and cumin and let stand for 10 minutes.

Cut the ham slices in half lengthwise, then wrap each slice around a fig half. Top with a basil leaf and secure with a toothpick. Arrange the wrapped figs on a platter or plate and serve within 1 hour of making.

CHAPTER 2

DIPS & SPREADS

This splendid selection of dips and spreads is very easy to prepare. From a smooth Avocado-Green Goddess Dip (page 31) to earthy versions of homemade hummus to a rich and nutty Romesco Spread (page 42), all of these recipes are meant to be served with fresh and crunchy crudités, crispy crackers and chips, and an assortment of breads and toasts.

AVOCADO-GREEN GODDESS DIP

SERVES 6 TO 8

2 anchovy fillets, drained and coarsely chopped

1 medium shallot, coarsely chopped

1 garlic clove, coarsely chopped

2 Tbsp fresh lemon juice

1 Tbsp white wine vinegar

1 large ripe avocado, peeled, pitted, and quartered

½ cup [120 g] sour cream

2 Tbsp chopped fresh flat-leaf parsley

2 Tbsp chopped fresh tarragon

2 Tbsp minced chives

1 tsp extra-virgin olive oil

Kosher salt and freshly ground black pepper

This creamy, velvety-smooth dip is made with a ripe avocado and garden-fresh herbs, and it tastes just as good as it looks. Try it with tortilla chips and raw vegetables or spread it on toasts. It would be lovely served with White Wine, Orange & Mint Sangria (page 181), and it's also nice with Albariño or Pinot Gris.

Place the anchovies, shallot, garlic, lemon juice, and vinegar in a food processor and blend until the shallot and garlic are finely chopped. Add the avocado, sour cream, parsley, tarragon, and chives and blend until smooth. Add the olive oil, season with salt and pepper, and blend again. Refrigerate for 1 hour before serving. This dip doesn't keep well and is best enjoyed the day it's made.

HERBED YOGURT DIP

SERVES 6 TO 8

1½ cups [360 g] Greek yogurt

½ tsp superfine sugar

¼ tsp ground cardamom

¼ tsp ground cumin

1 small jalapeño pepper, seeded and coarsely chopped

½ cup [20 g] chopped fresh flat-leaf parsley

½ cup [20 g] chopped fresh cilantro

1 Tbsp chopped fresh dill

1 Tbsp chopped fresh mint

1 Tbsp chopped fresh tarragon

¼ cup [60 ml] extra-virgin olive oil

1 Tbsp fresh lemon juice

Kosher salt and freshly ground pepper

Salted pistachio nuts, coarsely chopped, for garnish

When jalapeño peppers, fresh herbs, olive oil, and lemon are blended together and mixed into creamy Greek yogurt, they create an unbeatable flavor combination. Sauvignon Blanc or Vinho Verde from Portugal pair well with this tangy, refreshing dip.

In a medium bowl, combine the yogurt, sugar, cardamom, and cumin.

Place the jalapeño, parsley, cilantro, dill, mint, tarragon, olive oil, and lemon juice in a food processor and blend until smooth and incorporated. Season with salt and pepper and blend again.

Spoon the yogurt mixture into a shallow bowl, gently fold in the herb mixture, and stir well to combine. Cover and refrigerate for at least 1 hour before serving. Stir the dip again, garnish with the pistachios, and serve.

MAKE AHEAD: The dip will keep without the garnish, tightly covered in the refrigerator, for up to 1 day. Garnish just before serving.

SPICY CLAM DIP

SERVES 6 TO 8

12 cherrystone clams, rinsed well

1 cup [240 g] cream cheese, at room temperature

½ cup [120 g] low-fat sour cream

½ red bell pepper, stemmed, seeded, and finely diced

1 to 2 tsp hot sauce

1 tsp celery seed

Kosher salt and freshly ground black pepper

½ cup [20 g] chopped fresh flat-leaf parsley, for garnish

Here's a zesty dip that can be served at all types of parties, from backyard get-togethers to holiday soirées. Prepare it ahead of time and serve slightly chilled with chips, pita crisps, and fresh vegetables. It also makes a good stuffing for celery sticks. Serve this dip with a white wine that goes well with seafood, such as crisp Pinot Grigio or unoaked Chardonnay, or a light red like Lambrusco.

Place the clams in a large soup pot, add 2 cups [480 ml] of water, and bring to a boil. Cover and cook until the clams open, about 5 minutes. Drain the clams and let cool. Discard any clams that have not opened.

When cool enough to handle, remove the clams from their shells, coarsely chop them, and transfer to a food processor. Add the cream cheese, sour cream, bell pepper, hot sauce, and celery seed and blend in short pulses until the clams and bell pepper are finely chopped but the mixture is not too smooth. Season with salt and pepper and pulse again. Scrape the dip into a bowl, cover, and refrigerate for at least 1 hour before serving. Taste and adjust the seasoning, if necessary. Garnish with the parsley and serve.

MAKE AHEAD: The dip will keep without the garnish, tightly covered in the refrigerator, for up to 3 days. Garnish just before serving.

WARM SPINACH DIP

SERVES 6

2 Tbsp extra-virgin olive oil

1 small white onion, finely chopped

1 garlic clove, finely chopped

1½ lb [680 g] fresh spinach (about 3 bunches), trimmed and coarsely chopped

Kosher salt and freshly ground black pepper

½ cup [120 ml] whole milk

¾ cup [170 g] cream cheese, at room temperature

1 tsp Worcestershire sauce

Dash of hot sauce

¾ cup [60 g] shredded mozzarella cheese

¼ cup [8 g] freshly grated Parmesan cheese

Rich and cheesy, this scrumptious dish is best served hot out of the oven with warm crusty bread or potato chips. While it can be tricky to pair wine with vegetables like spinach or artichokes, dry white Muscadet or a low-tannic red, such as Chianti Classico, would be good choices.

Preheat the oven to 425°F [220°C]. Grease a shallow baking dish and set aside.

Heat the oil in a large skillet over medium heat. Add the onion and garlic and cook, stirring occasionally, until softened, about 5 minutes. Add the spinach and a generous amount of salt and pepper and cook, stirring, until the spinach is completely wilted. Transfer to a colander, drain, let cool, then squeeze out the excess liquid.

In a medium saucepan, bring the milk to a boil over medium heat. Turn the heat to low, add the cream cheese, and whisk it until melted and smooth. Add the drained spinach, Worcestershire sauce, and hot sauce and stir to blend. Taste and adjust the season-ing, if necessary.

Transfer the spinach mixture to the prepared baking dish and sprinkle with the mozzarella cheese. Bake for 15 minutes, then sprinkle with the Parmesan cheese. Bake until the top is bubbly and golden brown, 5 to 10 minutes more. Serve at once. This dish doesn't keep well and is best enjoyed the day it's made.

HERBED RICOTTA CHEESE SPREAD

SERVES 6 TO 8

1 lb [455 g] fresh whole-milk ricotta cheese

2 Tbsp whole milk

2 Tbsp extra-virgin olive oil, plus more for drizzling

2 tsp fresh lemon juice

1 tsp lemon zest

1 garlic clove, finely grated

½ cup [10 to 20 g] chopped fresh herbs, such as basil, chives, flat-leaf parsley, and tarragon

Kosher salt and freshly ground black pepper

This is a spread that you will want to serve with grilled bread and fresh tomatoes, or as a creamy addition on an antipasto plate loaded with salumi, olives, and crudités. It's delightful with sparkling rosé or Prosecco.

Place the ricotta, milk, olive oil, lemon juice, lemon zest, and garlic in a food processor and blend until very smooth. Transfer to a serving bowl, stir in the herbs, and season with salt and pepper. Before serving, drizzle the top of the spread with more olive oil.

MAKE AHEAD: The spread will keep, tightly covered in the refrigerator, for 1 day. Bring to room temperature before serving.

ROASTED RED PEPPER & HARISSA HUMMUS

SERVES 6 TO 8

One 15½ oz [445 g]
   can chickpeas,
   drained and rinsed

2 garlic cloves, coarsely
   chopped

½ cup [110 g] chopped
   roasted red peppers, plus
   more for garnish

¼ cup [60 ml] extra-virgin
   olive oil, plus more for
   garnish

2 Tbsp tahini

2 Tbsp fresh lemon juice

2 tsp harissa sauce
   (see Note), plus more
   as needed

Kosher salt and freshly
   ground black pepper

Toasted pine nuts, for
   garnish

Making hummus from scratch is very easy. It tastes so much better than store-bought and you can add a variety of ingredients to suit your taste. Harissa sauce is a great addition to hummus. This staple of North African and Middle Eastern cooking is a hot chile paste that is a blend of chile peppers, garlic, olive oil, and spices. Use it sparingly—a little goes a long way. Serve this hummus with rosé, Riesling, or Pinot Noir.

Place the chickpeas, garlic, peppers, oil, tahini, lemon juice, and harissa sauce in a food processor. Season with salt and pepper and blend until very smooth. Taste and adjust the seasoning, adding additional harissa sauce for more heat, if desired.

Garnish the hummus with chopped peppers, toasted pine nuts, and a drizzle of olive oil and serve.

MAKE AHEAD: The hummus will keep without the garnish, tightly covered in the refrigerator, for up to 3 days. Bring to room temperature and garnish before serving.

NOTE: Harissa sauce or paste can be found in Middle Eastern markets, the international section of supermarkets, or online.

ROASTED BEET HUMMUS

SERVES 6 TO 8

2 small red beets, trimmed

One 15½ oz [445 g]
　can chickpeas,
　drained and rinsed

3 Tbsp tahini

3 Tbsp extra-virgin olive oil

2 Tbsp fresh lemon juice

2 garlic cloves, coarsely
　chopped

½ tsp ground cumin

Kosher salt and freshly
　ground black pepper

½ cup [120 g] Greek yogurt

1 Tbsp prepared
　horseradish

Chopped fresh flat-leaf
　parsley, for garnish

Chopped fresh mint leaves,
　for garnish

This bright and vibrant version of hummus is made with roasted beets. Middle Eastern fare is very wine-friendly, and a number of wines, such as rosé, Riesling, or Pinot Noir, would pair well with this hummus spread.

Preheat the oven to 450°F [230°C].

Wrap the beets in aluminum foil, place them in a small roasting pan, and roast until fork-tender, 40 to 50 minutes.

When cool enough to handle, peel the skins off of the beets, cut the beets into small chunks, and transfer to a food processor. Add the chickpeas, tahini, olive oil, lemon juice, garlic, and cumin. Season with salt and pepper and blend until very smooth, adding 1 or 2 tablespoons of water if the mixture seems too thick. Taste and adjust the seasoning, if necessary.

In a small bowl, mix together the yogurt and horseradish. Transfer the hummus to a shallow serving bowl. Spoon the yogurt mixture over the top, garnish with parsley and mint, and serve.

MAKE AHEAD: The hummus will keep without the garnish, tightly covered in the refrigerator, for up to 3 days. Bring to room temperature and garnish before serving.

HUMMUS

Hummus, long a staple of Mediterranean cooking, is now very popular worldwide and it is certainly having its time in the sun, with creative renditions on menus everywhere. Because it lends itself to so many different spices, herbs, and flavor profiles, it's a great palette for experimentation. Some of my favorite ingredients to blend into hummus, other than those featured in the two recipes on pages 38–39 are black olives and roasted carrots and onions. Or take your plain hummus to the next level—and make it main-dish-worthy—by topping it with one of the following:

* Garlicky sautéed ground lamb

* A swirl of labneh and a sprinkle of chopped fresh mint

* A thick layer of olive oil and a sprinkling of za'atar

Or create tasty flatbreads and quesadillas with hummus:

* Spread it over warm flatbreads or pita and top with grilled vegetables and yogurt

* Spread it over tortillas with avocados, onions, and cheese and cook in a skillet or in the oven until the cheese is melted

EGGPLANT & CAPER SPREAD

SERVES 6 TO 8

2 lb [910 g] (about
    2 medium) eggplants,
    peeled and cut into 1 in
    [2.5 cm] cubes

3 garlic cloves, halved

4 Tbsp [60 ml] extra-virgin
    olive oil

Kosher salt and freshly
    ground black pepper

1 cup [40 g] chopped fresh
    flat-leaf parsley, plus
    more for garnish

½ cup [24 g] chopped
    green onions (white and
    green parts), plus more
    for garnish

2 Tbsp Greek yogurt

1 Tbsp drained capers

1 Tbsp fresh lemon juice

1 tsp lemon zest

½ tsp sweet paprika

Pinch of cayenne pepper

Toast or pita bread, for
    serving

Fresh lemon juice, zest, and salty capers enhance the flavor of mellow roasted eggplant in this spread. It's terrific to slather onto slices of toasted rustic bread or pita triangles. Along with a red Rioja or a chilled white Albariño, pungent kalamata olives and chopped fresh cucumbers are ideal accompaniments.

Preheat the oven to 400°F [200°C].

Toss the eggplant cubes and garlic with 3 tablespoons of the olive oil and a generous amount of salt and pepper. Arrange them on a baking sheet and roast until tender, about 20 minutes. Let cool.

Transfer the cooked eggplant and garlic to a food processor. Add the parsley, green onions, yogurt, capers, lemon juice, lemon zest, paprika, cayenne, and the remaining 1 tablespoon of olive oil and blend until smooth. Transfer to a bowl, cover, and refrigerate for about 2 hours.

Taste and adjust the seasoning, if necessary, garnish with parsley and green onions, and serve with toast.

MAKE AHEAD: The spread will keep, tightly covered in the refrigerator, for up to 3 days.

ROMESCO SPREAD

SERVES 10 TO 12

One 16 oz [455 g] jar roasted red peppers, seeded and chopped

¼ cup [60 ml] extra-virgin olive oil

2 Tbsp red wine vinegar

½ cup [60 g] slivered almonds, toasted

2 garlic cloves

1 tsp sweet smoked paprika

¾ tsp kosher salt

Pinch of cayenne pepper

Romesco sauce originated in Catalonia, Spain, where it was served as an accompaniment to grilled meat and fish. There are many ways to prepare this rich, flavorful condiment. I serve it as a spread for toasts with Manchego cheese and chopped green olives, and as a creamy accompaniment to sardines and anchovies. Any number of Spanish wines, such as Tempranillo, Rioja, or sparkling Cava, would complement this romesco beautifully.

Place the peppers, oil, vinegar, almonds, garlic, paprika, salt, and cayenne in a blender and blend until smooth. Taste and adjust the seasoning, if necessary, and use as a topping or serve with fresh vegetables for dipping.

MAKE AHEAD: The spread will keep, tightly covered in the refrigerator, for up to 1 week.

SMOKED TROUT SPREAD

SERVES 6 TO 8

8 oz [230 g] smoked trout
fillet, cut into small pieces
(see Note)

3/4 cup [180 g] fresh whole-
milk ricotta cheese

1/4 cup [60 g] low-fat sour
cream

2 green onions (white and
green parts), trimmed and
minced

2 Tbsp minced chives

1 Tbsp prepared
horseradish

1 tsp fresh lemon juice

Dash of hot sauce

Freshly ground black
pepper

Smoked trout blends beautifully with ricotta cheese and horseradish in this luscious spread. Serve it with crackers, rye or pumpernickel toasts, or rounds of fresh cucumber. Crisp Sauvignon Blanc or Pinot Grigio are good accompaniments to this rich and salty appetizer.

Place the smoked trout, ricotta, sour cream, green onions, chives, horseradish, lemon juice, and hot sauce in a food processor. Season with pepper and blend until smooth. Taste and adjust the seasoning, if necessary, and blend again. Scrape the mixture into a bowl, cover, and refrigerate for 2 to 3 hours before serving.

MAKE AHEAD: This spread will keep, tightly covered in the refrigerator, for up to 1 day.

NOTE: Smoked trout is available in fish markets and specialty shops where high-quality smoked fish is sold.

TUNA TAPENADE

SERVES 6 TO 8

½ cup [90 g] black olives, such as kalamata or Niçoise, drained, pitted, and chopped

½ cup [90 g] green olives, such as Castelvetrano or Cerignola, drained, pitted, and chopped

3 anchovy fillets, chopped, or 1 tsp anchovy paste

2 Tbsp chopped fresh flat-leaf parsley

2 Tbsp fresh lemon juice

1 Tbsp grated lemon zest

1 to 3 Tbsp extra-virgin olive oil

2 tsp drained capers

1 garlic clove, coarsely chopped

½ tsp Dijon mustard

One 5 to 6 oz [140 to 170 g] can oil-packed tuna, undrained

Freshly ground black pepper

This tasty version of the classic Mediterranean condiment, tapenade, is made with a blend of black and green olives, capers, anchovies, and canned tuna. It's fabulous served with crackers, toasts, or raw vegetables or spread onto a crusty baguette and topped with fresh tomatoes for a picnic lunch. It would be lovely with a glass of sparkling rosé or Champagne.

Place the black and green olives, anchovies, parsley, lemon juice, lemon zest, 1 tablespoon of the olive oil, the capers, garlic, and mustard in a food processor and blend until fairly smooth but still a bit chunky, adding up to 2 tablespoons more oil if needed. Transfer to a medium bowl.

Place the tuna and its oil in a small bowl and flake it with a fork. Fold it gently into the olive mixture until well mixed. Season with pepper and gently mix again. Cover and refrigerate for at least 1 hour before serving.

MAKE AHEAD: The tapenade will keep, tightly covered in the refrigerator, for up to 1 week.

CHAPTER 3

CHEESE

From elegant savory tarts to gooey grilled cheese sandwich bites to a board filled with enticing cheeses that vary in color, texture, and taste, cheese is an essential ingredient in any party spread. The range of wines to serve with cheese is wide—from light whites to rich reds.

GOAT CHEESE-STUFFED ENDIVE

SERVES 6 TO 8

½ cup [115 g] goat cheese, at room temperature

¼ cup [55 g] cream cheese, at room temperature

½ cup [60 g] walnuts, coarsely chopped

1 Tbsp fresh lemon juice

1 Tbsp minced fresh chives, plus more for garnish

1 Tbsp finely chopped fresh flat-leaf parsley

Kosher salt and freshly ground black pepper

20 to 24 green and/or red Belgian endive or chicory leaves (2 or 3 heads)

Crisp endive leaves filled with a mixture of creamy goat cheese, walnuts, and fresh herbs are a perfect finger food to serve at all types of parties. This is a basic recipe, but if you like, you can sub in a variety of sweet and savory ingredients for different fillings and garnishes. Look for red Belgian endive leaves to add even more color to the platter. Full-bodied whites like Chardonnay or Viognier go well with these.

Place the goat cheese, cream cheese, walnuts, lemon juice, chives, and parsley in a food processor, season with salt and pepper, and blend until very smooth. Transfer to a small bowl (see Make Ahead).

Spoon the mixture evenly into the endive leaves, garnish with chives (or other toppings and garnishes of your choice; see sidebar, page 50), and serve.

MAKE AHEAD: The goat cheese mixture will keep, tightly covered, in the refrigerator for up to 1 day. Bring to room temperature before serving.

MORE ENDIVE FILLINGS

* Orange segments, balsamic glaze; garnish with toasted nuts and chopped fresh flat-leaf parsley

* Chopped apples; garnish with toasted nuts and orange zest

* Chopped pears; garnish with toasted nuts and pomegranate seeds

* Spoonful of Plum & Ginger Jam (page 167) or apricot preserves

* Chopped roasted beets, balsamic glaze; garnish with toasted nuts

* Chopped smoked salmon; garnish with drained capers, lemon zest, and chopped dill

* Chopped kalamata olives; garnish with red pepper flakes and chopped fresh flat-leaf parsley

* Chopped fresh tomatoes; garnish with pine nuts and chopped basil

FRIED HALLOUMI CHEESE

SERVES 4 TO 6

8 oz [230 g] Halloumi
cheese

3 to 4 Tbsp extra-virgin
olive oil

Fresh lemon juice

Pinch of red pepper flakes

Freshly ground black
pepper

When served plain, Halloumi cheese is firm and has a salty but mild taste. But once it's fried or grilled, it becomes truly delicious. In this fabulous appetizer, cubed Halloumi cheese is fried and then drizzled with fresh lemon juice and olive oil. Serve it on its own or with hummus, olives, and pita. You can find Halloumi at stores that feature a wide variety of cheeses, specialty cheese shops, or Middle Eastern markets. It is also available online. This recipe can easily be doubled, but make sure that the Halloumi is fried in a single layer. A zippy white like Sauvignon Blanc or Vinho Verde is a good complement to this tangy dish.

Drain the Halloumi, slice the slab in half horizontally, then cut the cheese into batons and slice them into cubes. Pat the cubes very dry with paper towels.

Heat 2 tablespoons of the olive oil in a heavy skillet over medium heat. When hot, add the cheese cubes and cook for a few minutes without stirring, until the bottoms are well browned.

Turn the Halloumi cubes with a spatula and brown them on the other side, until they are golden-brown, 6 to 8 minutes total.

Transfer the fried Halloumi cubes to a bowl. Sprinkle them with lemon juice, red pepper flakes, and black pepper. Drizzle with 1 or 2 tablespoons more olive oil and serve warm or at room temperature.

BLACK BEAN, MUSHROOM & CHEESE QUESADILLAS WITH AVOCADO CREAM

SERVES 6 TO 8

AVOCADO CREAM:

1 ripe avocado, halved, pitted, peeled, and cut into small pieces

2 Tbsp fresh lime juice

2 Tbsp light sour cream or crème fraîche

Kosher salt

Hot sauce (optional)

QUESADILLAS:

One 15½ oz [445 g] can black beans, rinsed and drained

1¼ cups [110 g] freshly grated Monterey Jack cheese

1¼ cups [110 g] freshly grated yellow Cheddar cheese

These hearty vegetarian quesadillas feature a generous amount of cheese melted over black beans, red peppers, spinach, and mushrooms, and they are always a big crowd-pleaser. Serve them with silky-smooth avocado cream; it's a mouthwatering sauce that's good with tacos, sandwiches, and burgers as well. A Zinfandel would taste pretty great with these quesadillas.

To make the avocado cream: Place the avocado, lime juice, sour cream, salt to taste, and hot sauce (if using) in a food processor and pulse until very smooth. Cover and refrigerate until serving, but don't store it longer than a few hours.

To make the quesadillas: Place the beans in a medium shallow bowl. Mash them coarsely with a potato masher or the back of a spoon and set aside. Place the grated cheeses in a large bowl, stir together, and set aside.

2 Tbsp extra-virgin olive oil

1 small white onion, chopped

2 garlic cloves, thinly sliced

1 red bell pepper, stemmed, seeded, and finely chopped

4 oz [115 g] cremini mushrooms, stemmed and thinly sliced

2 cups [40 g] baby spinach

2 Tbsp chopped fresh cilantro

1 tsp ground cumin

1 tsp smoked paprika

Kosher salt and freshly ground black pepper

4 flour tortillas (8 in [20 cm] diameter)

Fresh lime wedges, for serving

Hot sauce, for serving

Heat the oil in a large skillet over medium heat.

Add the onion and cook until softened, about 5 minutes. Add the garlic and cook for 1 minute. Add the bell pepper and mushrooms and cook, stirring, until softened, about 5 minutes. Add the spinach and cook until wilted, about 3 minutes. Add the reserved beans, cilantro, cumin, and paprika, season with salt and pepper, and cook, stirring, until the mixture is softened, about 5 minutes.

Preheat the oven to 200°F [95°C].

To assemble the quesadillas, place 1 tortilla at a time on a work surface and sprinkle a layer of the cheese evenly over the tortilla. Cover the cheese with some of the black bean mixture and sprinkle with another layer of cheese. Top with another tortilla and press it down with a spatula.

Place a dry nonstick skillet over medium heat until very hot. Place a quesadilla in the skillet and cook, pressing down with the spatula, until lightly browned on the bottom, about 3 minutes. Flip the quesadilla and cook until lightly browned and the cheese is melted, about 3 minutes. Transfer the quesadilla to a baking sheet and keep it warm in the oven. Repeat with the remaining quesadillas.

To serve, cut each quesadilla into six pieces and serve with the avocado cream, lime wedges, and hot sauce.

MAKE AHEAD: The avocado cream will keep, tightly covered in the refrigerator, for about 2 hours. The quesadillas are best enjoyed the day they're made.

BLUE CHEESE GOUGÈRES

SERVES 6 TO 8

¼ cup [60 ml] dry white wine

4 Tbsp [55 g] unsalted butter, cubed

½ tsp freshly ground black pepper

¼ tsp kosher salt

⅔ cup [85 g] unbleached all-purpose flour

3 large eggs, at room temperature

⅓ cup [40 g] finely crumbled blue cheese

Gougères are perfect little bites to eat and enjoy with wine. These savory cheese puffs are delicately crisp on the outside, airy and tender on the inside, and loaded with flavor. Although they're most often made with Gruyère cheese, this version is made with tangy blue cheese. Try them with Champagne, Brut Rosé Cava from Spain, or Pinot Noir.

Preheat the oven to 375°F [190°C]. Line a large rimmed baking sheet with parchment paper.

In a medium saucepan, combine the wine, butter, pepper, and salt with ¼ cup [60 ml] of water. Bring to a boil over medium heat, stirring until the butter is melted. Stir in the flour and lower the heat to medium-low. Stir constantly until the mixture forms large dough clumps and a film forms on the bottom of the pan, about 1 minute. Remove from the heat and let cool for 5 minutes.

continued

In a medium bowl, whisk the eggs. Transfer 1 tablespoon of the beaten eggs to a small bowl and reserve. Add one-third of the remaining eggs to the dough and whisk until well incorporated. Add the remaining eggs in two additions, stirring until they are completely incorporated after each addition. Stir in the cheese.

Drop the dough mixture by teaspoonfuls onto the prepared baking sheet and space them about 1 inch [2.5 cm] apart. Brush each gougère with the reserved egg using a pastry brush. Bake until lightly browned and puffed, about 30 minutes. Serve hot, warm, or at room temperature.

MAKE AHEAD: The gougères can be made up to 1 week in advance. After they have cooled completely, store them in airtight containers in the freezer. To heat for serving, bake the gougères in a 375°F [190°C] oven until golden brown and baked through, about 25 minutes.

WARM PIMIENTO CHEESE SANDWICHES

2 cups [160 g] freshly grated sharp yellow Cheddar cheese

2 cups [160 g] freshly grated extra-sharp white Cheddar cheese

1/2 cup [110 g] drained pimientos or roasted red peppers, finely chopped

1/2 cup [120 g] mayonnaise

1 tsp fresh lemon juice

1 tsp Worcestershire sauce

Dash of hot sauce

1/2 tsp celery salt

Kosher salt and freshly ground black pepper

2 to 3 Tbsp unsalted butter, at room temperature

12 slices white or sourdough bread

In the South, pimiento cheese is an all-time party favorite that is served with crackers, chips, and celery. There are many variations and versions of this dip, but its main ingredients are sharp Cheddar cheese, mayonnaise, and pimientos. It makes a wonderful filling for warm cheese sandwiches, especially when they're baked until crispy on the outside and meltingly creamy on the inside. Any type of bubbly would be an excellent accompaniment.

Combine the grated cheeses and pimientos in a large bowl, toss together, and set aside. In a medium bowl, stir together the mayonnaise, lemon juice, Worcestershire sauce, and hot sauce until combined. Fold the mayonnaise mixture into the cheese mixture until combined. Add the celery salt, season with salt and pepper to taste, and stir. Cover and refrigerate for at least 2 hours.

continued

Preheat the oven to 425°F [220°C].

Butter one side of each slice of bread. Place 6 slices of the bread, buttered-side down, on a work surface. Spread the pimiento cheese over the slices and top with the remaining 6 slices of bread, buttered-side up.

Arrange the sandwiches on a large baking sheet and place them in the oven. Bake until the tops are golden brown, about 5 minutes. Using a spatula, turn the sandwiches and bake until golden brown on the second side and the cheese filling is soft and creamy, about 5 minutes. Cut each sandwich into quarters or triangles and serve at once.

MAKE AHEAD: The pimiento cheese filling will keep, tightly covered in the refrigerator, for up to 3 days.

ONION & GRUYÈRE TART

SERVES 6 TO 8

1 cup [140 g] unbleached all-purpose flour

6 Tbsp [85 g] cold unsalted butter, cut into ¼ in [6 mm] cubes

Kosher salt

3 to 6 Tbsp [45 to 90 ml] ice water

2 Tbsp extra-virgin olive oil

1 lb [455 g] yellow onions (about 4), peeled and thinly sliced

1 Tbsp sherry

Freshly ground black pepper

½ cup [60 g] freshly grated Gruyère or Comté cheese

1 Tbsp chopped fresh thyme, plus extra sprigs for garnish

This savory tart is made with slow-cooked caramelized onions that are sweetened with sherry and baked into a buttery crust with Gruyère cheese and fresh thyme. Serve it warm, cut into wedges, with a glass of wine before dinner. Champagne, Riesling, or a light-bodied, fruity Beaujolais would taste fantastic with the tart.

Place the flour, butter, and a pinch of salt in a food processor and pulse until the mixture resembles coarse meal. Add the ice water, 1 tablespoon at a time and pulsing between additions, until the dough just comes together. Form the dough into a ball and flatten it into a disk about 1 inch [2.5 cm] thick. Wrap in plastic wrap and refrigerate for 1 hour.

Heat the olive oil in a large skillet over medium-low heat. Add the onions and salt to taste and cook, stirring occasionally, until softened and golden brown, about 30 minutes. Lower the heat if the onions brown too quickly or stick to the bottom of the pan. Add the sherry and pepper to taste and cook, stirring, for 2 minutes. Remove the onions from the heat and let cool.

Preheat the oven to 375°F [190°C].

On a floured surface, roll out the dough with a rolling pin sprinkled with flour to fit in a 10 inch [25 cm] tart pan with a removable bottom. Add a bit more flour if the dough starts sticking to the pin or the work surface. Fit the dough into the pan, pressing it into the fluted edges, and trim off any excess pastry. Sprinkle half of the Gruyère over the bottom of the tart. Spoon the cooled onions into the shell and spread evenly over the cheese. Sprinkle the thyme over the onions, and then sprinkle the tart with the remaining cheese.

Bake until the crust and the onions are golden brown, 30 to 35 minutes. Remove from the oven and let cool slightly. Garnish with thyme sprigs and serve warm or at room temperature. This tart doesn't keep well and is best enjoyed the day it's made.

CHEDDAR-NUT WAFERS

SERVES 6 TO 8

1⅓ cups [185 g] unbleached all-purpose flour

1 cup [80 g] freshly grated sharp yellow Cheddar cheese

½ cup [15 g] freshly grated Parmesan cheese

1 tsp kosher salt

¼ tsp black pepper

Pinch of cayenne pepper

½ cup [110 g] cold unsalted butter, cut into small cubes

1 large egg yolk

¼ cup [30 g] pecans or walnuts, coarsely chopped

2 Tbsp ice water

It's always good to have a go-to recipe for an easy snack that can be served alongside cocktails, and these lovely wafers made with Cheddar and Parmesan cheese and chopped nuts are just the ticket. They pair well with Merlot, Côtes du Rhone, and sparkling rosé.

Place the flour, Cheddar, Parmesan, salt, pepper, and cayenne in the bowl of a food processor and pulse until combined. Add the butter to the mixture and pulse again to form coarse crumbs. Add the egg yolk, pecans, and ice water and pulse again to form a dough.

Turn the dough out onto a work surface and divide it into two equal pieces. Roll and shape each piece of dough into a 1 inch [2.5 cm] thick by 11 inch [28 cm] long log; wrap them in wax paper or parchment paper and refrigerate until the dough is firm, at least 2 hours or overnight (see Make Ahead).

Preheat the oven to 375°F [190°C]. Line two baking sheets with parchment paper and set aside.

Unwrap the dough and, using a sharp knife, slice each log crosswise into 1/4 inch [6 mm] thick rounds. Arrange the rounds on the prepared baking sheets with 1/2 inch [12 mm] of space between them.

Bake the wafers until crisp, 18 to 20 minutes, rotating the baking sheets halfway through baking. Let cool for 5 minutes on the baking sheets. Serve warm or at room temperature.

MAKE AHEAD: The wafers will keep, tightly covered at room temperature, for up to 1 week. The wrapped cylinders of dough can be frozen for up to 3 months.

THE CHEESE BOARD

Wine and cheese are natural partners, and serving a platter of sumptuous cheeses, fresh fruit, crusty bread, and other tasty accoutrements along with some well-chosen wines is a never-fail party idea.

Balance is the key when putting together a cheese platter. Serve three to six different cheeses that vary in size, shape, texture, and color. Look for cheeses with contrasting and distinctive flavors—one that's hard and salty, another that's soft and buttery, and one that's assertive and a bit stinky.

To gauge how much cheese you will need, a good rule of thumb is to serve 5 to 6 ounces [140 to 170 g] per person. Cheese should never be served cold—always serve it at room temperature. Cut it just before serving to avoid drying out.

In addition to cheese, serve a selection of fresh fruit, such as apples, pears, grapes, and figs; dried fruit, such as apricots, figs, and raisins; and an assortment of nuts, such as walnuts, almonds, and pistachios, to accompany cheese. Pickled and marinated foods are important additions too. Olives, pickles, and pickled vegetables (pages 88–92) are great choices and add bright pops of color and texture to the platter. And don't forget other savory accompaniments, such as spicy mustard and tapenade; sweet preserves, jams, and chutneys (pages 164–69); and honey. Round out the cheese platter with a variety of breads, pita, and crackers.

Choosing from the many types and categories of cheese on the market can be overwhelming. Seek out advice from a knowledgeable cheesemonger from a good market, if you can. The following pages provide a guide to different styles of cheese and their origins.

HARD CHEESES

Hard cheeses are often grated but can be cut into chunks for serving. Their salty flavor and granular texture go well with fresh fruit.

Aged Gouda: This cow's milk cheese from the Netherlands has a distinctive, sharp, somewhat sweet flavor.

Asiago: This Italian cow's milk cheese has a rich, nutty flavor and crumbly texture.

Parmigiano-Reggiano: This cow's milk cheese from Italy has a salty, nutty flavor and grainy texture.

FIRM CHEESES

This wide-ranging category includes cheeses from aged sheep's milk to Cheddar. Firm cheeses are ideal for slicing and go well with sausage and salumi.

Cheddar: This cow's milk cheese originated in England, but many different versions of it are now produced in countries all over the world. Its flavor profile ranges from rich and mellow to sharp and pungent.

Comté and Gruyère: These cow's milk cheeses from France have hearty, nutty flavors and are often used in cooking fondues, quiches, and tarts.

Emmental: This is a cow's milk cheese that comes from Switzerland and is the original "Swiss cheese." It's known for its subtle, sweet flavor, it melts well, and it's often used to make fondue.

Jarlsberg: This mild cow's milk cheese was originally produced in Norway, but it is now made in many other countries. It has a clean, rich, nutty flavor.

Manchego: This Spanish sheep's milk cheese has a piquant, nutty flavor and a firm, buttery texture.

SEMI-SOFT CHEESES

These are good melting cheeses with a fairly spreadable consistency. They should always be served at room temperature so that their smooth and buttery flavors shine. They pair well with pickles and mustard as well as sweet condiments, such as fruit preserves, jams, and honey.

Fontina: This cow's milk cheese originated in Italy, but other versions are produced in other countries. Italian Fontina has an earthy, pungent flavor. Fontina produced in Denmark and Sweden has a much milder flavor.

Morbier: An aromatic, nutty cow's milk cheese from France, Morbier is defined by the dark vein of vegetable ash that runs through its center.

Muenster: The flavor of this French cow's milk cheese ranges from mild to assertive. This style of cheese bears no resemblance to bland supermarket Muenster cheese.

Port du Salut: This cow's milk cheese from France has a mild, creamy flavor and a very smooth texture.

Reblochon: When perfectly ripe, this French cow's milk cheese has a mild, delicate flavor and creamy texture.

SOFT-RIPENED/BLOOMY CHEESES

Soft-ripened cheeses have edible white rinds and rich, creamy interiors. Here are a few buying tips: Look for cheese with a clean rind; if the rind has dark spots or a brownish tinge, it's past its prime. To check for ripeness, the cheese should feel supple, not stiff to the touch. Try to buy a whole wheel rather than a cut wedge, as your self-cut wedges will be fresher. These cheeses taste wonderful with fresh fruit, berries, and crusty bread and are also good ones to serve for dessert.

Brie: This popular French cow's milk cheese has a smooth and buttery flavor.

Camembert: This cheese is very similar to Brie, but its flavor is a bit more intense and pungent.

Robiola: This cheese from Italy is made from different proportions of cow, sheep, and goat milk. Its flavor is very smooth, creamy, and a bit sweet.

WASHED-RIND CHEESES

The rinds of these cheeses are orange or brown in color from being bathed in brine and other liquids. They have assertive, often stinky flavor profiles and creamy interiors. Simple accompaniments like bread, nuts, and fruit taste best with these cheeses.

Époisses: This cow's milk cheese from France has a strong aroma and a funky, fruity flavor.

Livarot: The interior flavor of this French cow's milk cheese is soft and creamy. The taste of its rind is stronger.

Taleggio: The flavor of this cow's milk cheese from Italy ranges from mild and a bit citrusy to pungent as it ages.

BLUE CHEESES

The flavors of blue cheeses range from soft, creamy, and mild to firm and intense. Their pungent, funky flavors may be an acquired taste for some. They're great to serve with salty crackers, nuts, and sweet fruits and also good to crumble into salads and dips.

Bleu de Bresse: A creamy and mild cow's milk cheese from France.

Cabrales: This Spanish blue cheese is made with cow's milk or a mixture of cow, sheep, and goat milk and has a sharp, tangy flavor.

Gorgonzola: This cow's milk cheese from Italy is robust and strong-flavored with a rich aroma.

Maytag Blue: Produced in Iowa, this cow's milk blue cheese has a slightly tangy flavor with a lemony finish and a crumbly texture.

Roquefort: This aged sheep's milk cheese from France is sharp, salty, and slightly tangy with a creamy, crumbly texture.

Stilton: This assertive blue-mold cow's milk cheese is from England. It has a very rich and strong flavor and aftertaste.

DOUBLE- AND TRIPLE-CRÈME CHEESES

These luscious cow's milk cheeses are enriched with cream. Double-crème cheeses contain a minimum of 60 percent butterfat, and triple-crèmes have at least 75 percent. These soft and subtly sweet cheeses are delicate, so it is best to buy them whole instead of in cuts. These cheeses pair well with fresh fruits, honey, jams, and marmalades.

Brillat-Savarin: This French triple-crème cheese is very dense and buttery.

Délice de Bourgogne: This triple-crème cow's milk cheese from France is made with whole milk and crème fraîche. It has a tangy and buttery flavor.

L'Explorateur: This French triple-crème has a delightfully smooth flavor and a rich, buttery texture.

Saint-André: This creamy, buttery triple-crème from France has a mildly sweet finish.

CHÈVRES

Goat cheese, also known as chèvre, has a distinctive tart and tangy flavor. In addition to well-known French chèvres, such as Bucheron and Montrachet, there are many farmstead goat cheeses being produced domestically. These tangy cheeses are very good to serve with olives, capers, fresh herbs, and fruity olive oil, as well as figs and nuts.

Bucheron: This white, log-shaped chèvre has a smooth texture and medium-tart, lemony flavor.

Crottin: This well-known button-shaped cheese has a smooth and rich flavor and a rather nutty finish.

Montrachet: This smooth, white chèvre has a mildly tangy flavor and a creamy texture.

Domestic Fresh Chèvres: Many small farms from regions all over the country are producing excellent handcrafted fresh goat cheeses. A few good ones to seek out are Cypress Grove and Laura Chenel, from California; Coach Farm, from New York; Vermont Creamery and Consider Bardwell, from Vermont; and Goat Lady Dairy, from North Carolina.

FRESH CHEESES

These cheeses are made from fresh curds that have not been pressed or aged, so they should be eaten well within their "sell-by" dates. Their mild and savory flavors go very well with olive oil and fresh tomatoes and herbs, as well as salty meats like prosciutto and salami.

Burrata: *Burrata* means "buttery" in Italian. Its outside shell is made of a buffalo or cow's milk mozzarella, and its interior is a mixture of curds and cream. This very fresh cheese should be served at room temperature and does not last long.

Feta: Made from goat and sheep milk, this historically Greek cheese is tangy, somewhat salty, and has a creamy and almost crumbly texture.

Mozzarella: This cheese originated in Italy and was once made from the milk of water buffalo, but today it is made from cow's milk. It is best eaten fresh, within a few hours after it's made.

Ricotta: This fresh Italian cheese is made from sheep, cow, goat, or buffalo milk whey left over from the production of cheese. It is very smooth and spreadable and has a mildly sweet taste.

CHAPTER 4

VEGETABLES

No longer relegated to the crudité plate, vegetables have become popular stars of the buffet table. Whether they're served grilled, roasted, pickled, or raw, fresh vegetables will add beautiful crunch, color, and flavor and lighten up any type of spread.

GRILLED ASPARAGUS & PROSCIUTTO

SERVES 6 TO 8

2 lb [910 g] fresh asparagus, trimmed

¼ cup [60 ml] extra-virgin olive oil, plus more for brushing

1 Tbsp finely minced shallot

1 tsp white wine vinegar

1 tsp fresh lemon juice

8 oz [230 g] prosciutto, thinly sliced lengthwise

Nothing beats the flavor of nicely charred asparagus spears cooked on the grill, and they taste especially good wrapped in slices of salty prosciutto. For easier grilling and a juicier taste, use thick spears instead of thin ones. Pairing wines with asparagus can be tricky, but either a light-bodied Pinot Noir or a crisp Pinot Grigio would fit the bill here.

Lightly brush the asparagus with olive oil and set aside.

In a small bowl, whisk together the shallot, vinegar, and lemon juice. Whisk in the olive oil until smooth. Set aside.

Prepare a charcoal or gas grill for medium-high heat. Grill the asparagus, turning occasionally, until lightly charred, about 8 minutes. Remove from the heat and let cool a bit. Cut the asparagus spears in half if they seem too large for serving.

Wrap each asparagus spear with a strip of prosciutto and transfer to a platter. Drizzle lightly with the vinaigrette and serve. This dish doesn't keep well and is best enjoyed the day it's made.

GRILLED SHISHITO PEPPER SKEWERS

SERVES 6

30 shishito peppers, stems trimmed

Olive oil cooking spray

Kosher salt

1/2 cup [60 g] freshly grated queso fresco

1/2 tsp crushed red pepper flakes (see Note)

6 lime wedges, for garnish

Shishito peppers make a great snack and they taste rather sweet when grilled. These peppers are mild for the most part, but about one in ten of them is very spicy, with heat similar to that of a jalapeño. For easier grilling, it's best to thread the peppers on double rows of skewers. Shiraz and Zinfandel complement grilled spicy foods very well and they would be good choices here.

Soak 12 bamboo skewers in cold water for at least 30 minutes. Prepare a charcoal or gas grill for medium-high heat.

Thread 5 shishito peppers crosswise on a double row of skewers. Spray the peppers with olive oil cooking spray and sprinkle with salt. Grill the peppers, turning occasionally, until blistered, 6 to 8 minutes. Transfer to a serving platter. Sprinkle with the queso fresco and red pepper flakes and serve with the lime wedges. This dish doesn't keep well and is best enjoyed the day it's made.

NOTE: For a finer consistency, crush the red pepper flakes in a spice grinder or with a mortar and pestle.

GRILLED SNOW PEA SKEWERS

SERVES 6

8 oz [230 g] fresh snow
  peas

Extra-virgin olive oil, for
  drizzling

Pinch of kosher salt

Pinch of lemon pepper

Lemon or lime zest, for
  garnish

These snow peas deliver a good charred flavor from the grill and they have a nice, bright finish from a sprinkle of lemon pepper and citrus zest. Chilled dry sake would be a wonderful accompaniment.

Soak 12 bamboo skewers in cold water for at least 30 minutes. Prepare a charcoal or gas grill for medium-high heat.

Thread about 10 snow peas crosswise on a double row of skewers. Grill the snow peas, turning occasionally, until lightly browned and tender, 7 to 10 minutes. Transfer to a serving platter. Drizzle with olive oil, sprinkle with salt, lemon pepper, and lemon zest, and serve. This dish doesn't keep well and is best enjoyed the day it's made.

ROASTED VEGETABLE, MUSHROOM & HERB FRITTATA

SERVES 8 TO 10

1 red bell pepper, seeded and cut into 1/2 in [12 mm] pieces

1 yellow bell pepper, seeded and cut into 1/2 in [12 mm] pieces

1 small red onion, cut into 1/2 in [12 mm] pieces

2 Tbsp extra-virgin olive oil

Kosher salt and freshly ground black pepper

2 garlic cloves, thinly sliced

1 1/2 Tbsp unsalted butter

8 oz [230 g] shiitake mushrooms, stemmed and finely chopped

1/2 cup [20 g] chopped fresh flat-leaf parsley

2 Tbsp minced green onions (white and green parts)

2 Tbsp chopped fresh mint leaves

Here's a versatile frittata that makes a tasty appetizer to serve warm or at room temperature. This egg dish is usually baked in a round skillet, but using a rectangular baking dish makes it very easy to cut into small squares. The perfect thing to drink with this frittata is Champagne or a sparkling wine cocktail, such as an Autumn Bellini (page 174).

Preheat the oven to 425°F [220°C]. Butter a 9 by 13 inch [23 by 33 cm] baking dish and set aside.

Place the bell peppers and onion on a rimmed baking sheet. Drizzle with the olive oil, season with salt and pepper, and toss well to coat the vegetables. Bake for 15 minutes. Add the garlic, toss again, and bake for 10 minutes. Remove from the oven and lower the heat to 350°F [180°C].

Meanwhile, heat 1 tablespoon of the butter in a medium skillet over medium-high heat. Add the mushrooms and cook, stirring occasionally, until they are lightly browned and softened, about 5 minutes. Add the remaining 1/2 tablespoon butter to the pan and stir. Add the parsley, green onions, and mint, season with salt and pepper, and cook, stirring, for 1 minute. Remove from the heat and set aside.

10 extra-large eggs, at
room temperature

½ cup [120 ml] heavy
cream

½ cup [40 g] freshly
grated Gruyère cheese

½ cup [15 g] freshly
grated Parmesan cheese

Pinch of nutmeg

In a large bowl, whisk together the eggs, cream, half of the cheeses, and the nutmeg until combined. Add the roasted vegetables and the mushroom mixture to the egg mixture and gently stir.

Pour into the prepared baking dish and transfer to the oven. Bake until the frittata is puffed and set in the middle, 20 to 25 minutes. Sprinkle the top with the remaining cheeses and bake for 5 minutes, until the cheese is melted.

Let the frittata cool a bit, cut into squares, and serve warm or at room temperature.

MAKE AHEAD: The frittata can be made a few hours ahead of time if you're planning to serve it at room temperature.

ROASTED CAULIFLOWER WITH OLIVE & CAPER SAUCE

SERVES 6 TO 8

1 large cauliflower head, cut into florets

3/4 cup [180 ml] extra-virgin olive oil

Kosher salt and freshly ground black pepper

Zest of 1 lemon

2 garlic cloves, thinly sliced

1/4 cup [35 g] kalamata olives, pitted and halved

2 Tbsp drained capers

1 Tbsp chopped fresh thyme leaves

This preparation shows off the rich and nutty taste that develops when cauliflower is roasted. Serve it warm or at room temperature drizzled with lemony olive and caper sauce. A crisp white wine like Vernaccia tastes terrific with this surprisingly elegant snack.

Preheat the oven to 375°F [190°C].

Arrange the florets on a large rimmed baking sheet. Pour half of the olive oil over them, season generously with salt and pepper, and stir to coat. Roast until browned and tender, 35 to 40 minutes. Remove from the oven and let cool a bit.

In a small saucepan over medium-low heat, combine the remaining olive oil, the lemon zest, garlic, olives, capers, and thyme and cook, stirring occasionally, for 10 minutes.

Transfer the cauliflower to a serving bowl or platter. Drizzle with the sauce and serve with toothpicks or small forks. This dish doesn't keep well and is best enjoyed the day it's made.

ZUCCHINI FRITTERS

SERVES 4 TO 6

3 medium zucchini, peeled and shredded

Kosher salt

3 eggs, lightly beaten

1 Tbsp extra-virgin olive oil

½ cup [60 g] crumbled feta cheese

¼ cup [8 g] freshly grated Parmesan cheese

2 green onions (white and green parts), trimmed and minced

1 tsp paprika

Dash of hot sauce

Freshly ground black pepper

½ cup [70 g] all-purpose unbleached flour

1 tsp baking powder

½ cup [120 ml] corn, canola, or safflower oil, for frying

The trick to making crisp fritters is to squeeze all the moisture out of the zucchini before mixing it with the other ingredients. This requires the use of a thirsty kitchen towel and some elbow grease—but the results are well worth it. They're very good served with Avocado–Green Goddess Dip (page 31) and Herbed Yogurt Dip (page 32). Bright and acerbic Sauvignon Blanc pairs perfectly with the fritters and dips.

Put the zucchini in a colander, sprinkle generously with salt, and let drain for 30 minutes. Transfer to a clean kitchen towel and squeeze out as much moisture as possible.

In a large mixing bowl, combine the zucchini and eggs. Add the olive oil, feta, Parmesan, green onions, paprika, and hot sauce. Season with salt and pepper and mix well with a fork.

Sift the flour and baking powder together, stir into the zucchini mixture, and mix well.

Heat half of the corn oil in a large heavy skillet over medium heat until hot but not smoking. Drop a few heaping tablespoons of the zucchini batter into the pan, allowing room for them to spread. They should be about 3 inches [7.5 cm] in diameter. Fry until lightly browned on one side. Flip and fry until lightly browned and crisp on the other side, 6 to 8 minutes total.

Transfer to a plate lined with paper towels and keep warm in a low oven while cooking the remaining fritters. Continue frying with the remaining batter, adding more oil to the pan as needed. Serve at once.

PICKLED VEGETABLES

Crisp pickled vegetables are sensational to have on hand. They add vibrant crunch and color to rich appetizers, and because of their acidity and tanginess, they are perfect complements to cheese and charcuterie plates. Since they will keep in the refrigerator for weeks, they are always ready to serve at a moment's notice.

Here is a selection of vegetables for quick pickling—feel free to try others, especially when local gardens, greenmarkets, and farm stands are abundant with fresh produce. The yield for each of these recipes is 1 pint [455 g], but they can easily be doubled. For easier handling, be sure to use widemouthed jars.

Because pickles and wine both have high acidity, they aren't always compatible, but Prosecco and dry Riesling are very good options to pair with pickles.

PICKLED CAULIFLOWER

MAKES 1 PT [455 G]

½ cup [120 ml] white or apple cider vinegar

2 tsp kosher salt

1 tsp sugar

2 cups [455 g] cauliflower florets

1 small lemon, sliced into thin rounds

1 garlic clove, thinly sliced

½ tsp whole black peppercorns

½ tsp mustard seeds

In a large saucepan over high heat, combine 1 cup [240 ml] of water, the vinegar, salt, and sugar and bring to a boil, stirring to dissolve the salt and sugar. Add the cauliflower and stir until the brine returns to a boil. Remove from the heat and let cool.

Place 2 slices of lemon in the bottom of a clean 1 pint [455 g] jar and top with the garlic, peppercorns, and mustard seeds.

Using tongs or a slotted spoon, pack the cauliflower into the jar. Pour the brine over the cauliflower, almost filling the jar, and place 2 slices of lemon on top of the cauliflower. Gently tap the jar a few times to remove any air bubbles. Cover tightly and let cool to room temperature. Refrigerate for at least 1 day before serving.

MAKE AHEAD: The pickled cauliflower will keep, tightly covered in the refrigerator, for up to 1 month.

PICKLED RED ONIONS

MAKES 1 PT [455 G]

½ cup [120 ml] white or apple cider vinegar

2 tsp honey

1 tsp kosher salt

1 tsp whole black peppercorns

1 tsp mustard seeds

½ tsp red pepper flakes

1 bay leaf

1 medium red onion, thinly sliced

In a small saucepan over high heat, combine ½ cup [120 ml] of water, the vinegar, honey, salt, peppercorns, mustard seeds, red pepper flakes, and bay leaf and bring to a boil, stirring to dissolve the honey. Add the onion and stir. Lower the heat to medium and simmer for 1 minute. Remove from the heat and let the onions and brine cool in the pan.

Using tongs or a slotted spoon, transfer the onions to a clean 1 pint [455 g] jar. Discard the bay leaf and pour the brine and the remaining solids over the onions, filling the jar. Gently tap the jar a few times to remove any air bubbles. Cover tightly and let cool to room temperature. Refrigerate for at least 2 hours before serving.

MAKE AHEAD: The pickled onions will keep, tightly covered in the refrigerator, for up to 2 weeks.

PICKLED GREEN BEANS

MAKES 1 PT [455 G]

6 oz [170 g] green beans

1 garlic clove, thinly sliced

½ tsp whole black
   peppercorns

½ tsp coriander seeds

1 small dried chile

1 bay leaf

1 cup [240 ml] white
   vinegar

½ cup [120 ml] white wine

1 Tbsp sugar

1 tsp kosher salt

Before you trim the beans, arrange them vertically in a clean 1 pint [455 g] jar to see how they will fit. Trim them to fit, leaving at least ½ inch [12 mm] of space at the top of the jar. Pack the trimmed beans back into the jar. Add the garlic, peppercorns, coriander seeds, chile, and bay leaf to the jar.

In a small saucepan over high heat, combine the vinegar, wine, sugar, and salt and bring to a boil, stirring to dissolve the salt and sugar. Remove from the heat.

Pour the brine over the beans, filling the jar to within ½ inch [12 mm] of the top. Gently tap the jar a few times to remove any air bubbles. Cover tightly and let cool to room temperature. Refrigerate for at least 1 day before serving.

MAKE AHEAD: The pickled beans will keep, tightly covered in the refrigerator, for up to 1 month.

PICKLED FENNEL

MAKES 1 PT [455 G]

1 fennel bulb, trimmed and sliced into thin quarters

1 garlic clove, thinly sliced

2 fresh thyme sprigs

2 fresh rosemary sprigs

1 tsp dried mixed herbs, such as fines herbes or herbes de Provençe

1 tsp whole black peppercorns

1 tsp fennel seed

½ cup [120 ml] white or apple cider vinegar

1 Tbsp kosher salt

1 Tbsp sugar

Place the fennel, garlic, fresh and dried herbs, peppercorns, and fennel seed in a clean 1 pint [455 g] jar.

In a small saucepan over high heat, combine ¾ cup [180 ml] of water, the vinegar, salt, and sugar and bring to a boil, stirring to dissolve the salt and sugar. Remove from the heat.

Pour the brine over the fennel mixture, filling the jar to within ½ inch [12 mm] of the top. Gently tap the jar a few times to remove any air bubbles. Cover tightly and let cool to room temperature. Refrigerate for at least 2 days before serving.

MAKE AHEAD: The pickled fennel will keep, tightly covered in the refrigerator, for up to 1 month.

CHAPTER 5

BRUSCHETTA & TOASTS

Bruschetta and toasts are sublime snacks that are easy to serve and pair beautifully with any number of wines. You can create toppings with simple ingredients, such as canned beans and peppers, or more extravagant ones, such as fresh crabmeat and smoked salmon. Made with perfectly grilled or toasted bread, they're always fun to prepare.

GRILLING BREAD

Bruschetta, crostini, or toasts—whatever you want to you call them—are a favorite appetizer to serve for all occasions. When bread is grilled over a fire or on a grill pan or baked in the oven, its flavor and texture are enhanced, and any topping you might want to add will taste even more delicious. When preparing grilled bread, be sure to use artisanal loaves, such as ciabatta, sourdough, or baguettes—these hold up the best to grilling, and their flavor will complement the chosen toppings wonderfully.

Grill Method: Prepare a medium-hot fire for direct grilling in a charcoal barbecue or preheat a gas grill to medium-high. Cut bread into 1/2 inch [12 mm] slices or rounds and brush each side with olive oil. Arrange them in a single layer on the grill rack and grill, turning once, until they are golden brown, crispy, and slightly charred around the edges, 2 to 3 minutes per side. Transfer the bread to a platter and rub one side of each slice with the cut side of half of a garlic clove, if desired.

Grill Pan Method: Heat an ungreased stove-top grill pan over medium heat. Cut bread into 1/2 inch [12 mm] slices or rounds and brush each side with olive oil. Arrange them in a single layer on the pan and grill, turning once, until they are golden brown, crispy, and slightly charred around the edges, 4 to 5 minutes per side. Transfer the bread to a platter and rub one side of each slice with the cut side of half of a garlic clove, if desired.

Oven Method: Preheat the oven to 450°F [230°C]. Cut bread into 1/2 inch [12 mm] slices or rounds and brush one side with olive oil. Arrange them in a single layer on a baking sheet and bake, turning once, until golden brown and crispy, about 3 minutes per side. Transfer the bread to a platter and rub one side of each slice with the cut side of half of a garlic clove, if desired.

CANNELLINI & RED PEPPER BRUSCHETTA

SERVES 6 TO 8

3 Tbsp extra-virgin olive oil, plus more for drizzling

2 garlic cloves, minced

1 Tbsp finely chopped fresh thyme

Two 15 oz [420 g] cans cannellini beans, rinsed and drained

1½ Tbsp fresh lemon juice

1 Tbsp lemon zest

2 Tbsp finely chopped fresh flat-leaf parsley, plus extra leaves for garnish

Kosher salt and freshly ground black pepper

16 slices grilled bread (see page 96)

½ cup [110 g] roasted red or piquillo peppers, drained and thinly sliced

This tasty recipe uses ingredients that most everyone has on hand—a few cans of white beans, a jar of red peppers, garlic, lemon, and parsley—so it's quite easy to prepare for an impromptu get-together. Try this recipe with a glass of rosé.

In a large skillet, heat 2 tablespoons of the olive oil over medium heat. Add the garlic and thyme and cook until the garlic is fragrant and begins to soften, 2 to 3 minutes. Add the beans, lemon juice, and lemon zest and cook, stirring occasionally, for 5 minutes.

Transfer the mixture to a large bowl. Mash about half of the beans with a potato masher or a fork, leaving some of the beans whole for a bit of texture. Add the remaining 1 tablespoon of oil and the parsley. Season with salt and pepper and stir to combine.

Spoon the topping onto the grilled bread. Top with the red peppers, garnish with parsley leaves, drizzle with olive oil, and serve.

MAKE AHEAD: The bean spread will keep, tightly covered in the refrigerator, for up to 2 days. Bring to room temperature and adjust the seasoning, if necessary, before serving. The grilled bread can be prepared about 1 hour ahead of time.

RICOTTA, PROSCIUTTO & OLIVE BRUSCHETTA

SERVES 6 TO 8

3/4 cup [105 g] mixed olives, pitted and chopped

1 Tbsp extra-virgin olive oil

1 Tbsp drained capers

1 tsp lemon zest

Pinch of red pepper flakes

12 slices grilled bread (see page 96)

1 1/2 cups [360 g] fresh ricotta cheese

4 oz [115 g] prosciutto, thinly sliced lengthwise

Here's a great way to serve bruschetta: Top grilled bread with creamy ricotta cheese, a chunky mixture of black and green olives, capers, and lemon zest and a slice of prosciutto. If you prefer to make it vegetarian, simply omit the prosciutto. An Italian white, such as Pinot Grigio, or a red Chianti will complement the toasts beautifully.

In a medium bowl, combine the olives, olive oil, capers, lemon zest, and red pepper flakes and toss to mix well.

Spread each bread slice with some of the ricotta cheese, top with a spoonful of the olive mixture and a slice of prosciutto, and serve at once.

MAKE AHEAD: The grilled bread can be prepared about 1 hour ahead of time.

GOAT CHEESE & CARAMELIZED LEEK BRUSCHETTA

SERVES 6 TO 8

2 Tbsp extra-virgin olive oil

2 large leeks, trimmed, rinsed, and sliced into 2 in [5 cm] pieces

Kosher salt and freshly ground black pepper

12 slices grilled bread (see page 96)

6 oz [170 g] fresh goat cheese, at room temperature

Fresh lemon juice, for serving

Red pepper flakes, for serving

Slow-cooked leeks taste wonderful and their earthy-but-sweet flavor complements tangy, fresh goat cheese nicely. Here is a simple preparation for bruschetta that is topped with both. Either a crisp white Muscadet or a fruity red Pinot Noir would taste very good with these toasts.

In a large skillet, heat the olive oil over medium-high heat. Add the leeks, season with salt and pepper, and cook, stirring, until the leeks are well coated. Lower the heat to low and cook, stirring often, until the leeks are very soft and caramelized. Make sure the leeks don't stick to the bottom of the pan or brown too quickly. Remove the pan from the heat.

Spread each bread slice with the goat cheese and top with a spoonful of the leeks. Sprinkle the toasts with lemon juice and red pepper flakes and serve at once.

MAKE AHEAD: The grilled bread can be prepared about 1 hour ahead of time.

ROASTED FIG & MASCARPONE BRUSCHETTA

SERVES 6 TO 8

8 oz [230 g] fresh figs (about 6) stemmed and halved

2 Tbsp extra-virgin olive oil

2 Tbsp balsamic vinegar

1 Tbsp honey

1 Tbsp chopped fresh rosemary, plus more sprigs for garnish

12 slices grilled bread (see page 96)

½ cup [120 g] mascarpone cheese, at room temperature

Fresh figs have a very short growing season that usually runs from midsummer to fall, so it's best to make the most of them while you can. They are quite wonderful when roasted in a balsamic vinaigrette and paired with smooth and creamy mascarpone cheese. Try this bruschetta with Prosecco or a dry Lambrusco.

Preheat the oven to 450°F [230°C].

Arrange the figs, cut-side up, in a baking dish.

In a small bowl, whisk together the oil, vinegar, honey, and rosemary. Drizzle the mixture evenly over the top of the figs. Roast for 10 minutes, until the figs begin to brown. Remove from the oven and let cool a bit.

Spread each bread slice with the mascarpone and top with a roasted fig. Garnish with a rosemary sprig and serve.

MAKE AHEAD: The grilled bread can be prepared about 1 hour ahead of time.

CHICKEN LIVER PÂTÉ TOASTS WITH RED ONION SAUCE

SERVES 6 TO 8

CHICKEN LIVER PÂTÉ:

1 lb [455 g] chicken livers, trimmed

2 cups [480 ml] whole milk

6 Tbsp [85 g] unsalted butter, cut into cubes, at room temperature

2 shallots, finely chopped

1 Tbsp chopped fresh thyme

⅓ cup [80 ml] Madeira or port

Kosher salt and freshly ground black pepper

This smooth and silky pâté is very easy and inexpensive to make but it tastes luxurious. Because it is so rich, I like to serve it on small triangles of toasted pumpernickel bread. A Gigondas or a Côtes du Rhône would be an ideal pairing with these toasts.

To make the pâté: Place the chicken livers in a large bowl and add the milk. Soak the livers for 1 hour, drain and discard the milk, and pat dry.

In a large skillet over medium heat, melt 4 tablespoons [55 g] of the butter. Add the shallots and cook until translucent, making sure they don't brown. Add the livers, thyme, and Madeira and increase the heat to medium-high. Cook, stirring and turning occasionally, until the wine has reduced and the livers are lightly browned but still soft and pink on the inside, 6 to 8 minutes. Remove from the heat and let cool.

RED ONION SAUCE:

2 large red onions, cut into
  ¼ in [6 mm] dice

1½ cups [360 ml] chicken
  broth

½ cup [120 ml] dry sherry

2 Tbsp balsamic vinegar

1 Tbsp sugar

Kosher salt and freshly
  ground black pepper

¼ cup [60 g] crème fraîche,
  low-fat sour cream, or
  plain yogurt

6 slices grilled or toasted
  pumpernickel bread (see
  page 96), for serving

2 Tbsp drained capers, for
  garnish

To make the red onion sauce: In a saucepan over high heat, mix together the onions, broth, sherry, vinegar, and sugar and bring to a boil. Turn the heat to low and simmer, uncovered, for 40 to 45 minutes, stirring occasionally, until most of the liquid evaporates. Season with salt and pepper.

Stir in the crème fraîche and cook over very low heat for about 10 minutes more, until the flavors blend (see Make Ahead).

Spread the pâté over each bread slice, and using a sharp knife, cut each slice into four triangles. Top each triangle with some of the onion sauce, garnish with some of the capers, and serve.

MAKE AHEAD: The pâté will keep, tightly covered in the refrigerator, for up to 5 days. Bring to room temperature before serving.

The sauce will keep, tightly covered in the refrigerator, for up to 1 week. Bring to room temperature before serving. Serve it warm, if desired.

SMOKED SALMON TOASTS WITH WATERCRESS SAUCE

SERVES 6 TO 8

WATERCRESS SAUCE:

1 cup [34 g] coarsely chopped and stemmed watercress

2 garlic cloves, coarsely chopped

1 Tbsp whole-grain mustard

1 tsp Dijon mustard

2 Tbsp heavy cream

2 Tbsp extra-virgin olive oil

Kosher salt and freshly ground black pepper

½ cup [120 g] sour cream

SMOKED SALMON TOASTS:

6 slices grilled or toasted pumpernickel bread (see page 96)

8 oz [230 g] smoked salmon, cut into thin slices

4 to 6 hard-boiled eggs, cut into thin rounds

1 red onion, thinly sliced, for garnish

Minced fresh chives, for garnish

Freshly ground black pepper

Smoked salmon is an elegant addition to any party spread. Here, it is served on small toasts with creamy watercress sauce, slices of hard-boiled eggs, and chives. You will want to serve Champagne, Cava, or Prosecco with these delectable bites.

To make the watercress sauce: Put the watercress, garlic, mustards, cream, and olive oil in a food processor and season with salt and pepper. Blend until very smooth, scraping down the mixture as needed.

Transfer the mixture to a medium bowl. Add the sour cream and mix to combine. Cover and refrigerate for at least 1 hour before serving.

To prepare the toasts: Spoon the watercress sauce onto each bread slice, and using a sharp knife, cut each slice into four triangles. Arrange the salmon and egg slices on top of them. Top each triangle with a slice of red onion, sprinkle with chives and pepper, and serve.

MAKE AHEAD: The watercress sauce will keep, tightly covered in the refrigerator, for up to 3 days. Stir well before serving.

CRAB & AVOCADO TOASTS

SERVES 6

8 oz [230 g] cooked jumbo or backfin lump crabmeat

2¹/₂ Tbsp fresh lime juice

2 Tbsp mayonnaise

Pinch of cayenne pepper

Kosher salt and freshly ground black pepper

4 slices grilled or toasted Pullman or sourdough bread (see page 96)

2 Tbsp chopped fresh mint

1 avocado, halved, pitted, peeled, and cut into small slices

Freshly ground lemon pepper (optional)

When you're feeling extravagant and want to spring for fresh crabmeat, make these delicious little toasts for your guests. I like to finish them with a bit of lemon pepper to brighten the flavor of the crab spread. These are lovely with Pinot Blanc or a sparkling wine.

In a medium bowl, gently combine the crabmeat, lime juice, mayonnaise, and cayenne. Season with salt and pepper. Cover and refrigerate for 1 hour or up to overnight.

Spoon the crab mixture onto each bread slice, and using a sharp knife, cut each slice into four triangles. Garnish with the mint and top with a slice of avocado. Sprinkle with lemon pepper (if using) and serve.

MAKE AHEAD: The crab mixture will keep, tightly covered in the refrigerator, for 1 day. Mix well before assembling the toasts.

TOMATO TOASTS
WITH SERRANO HAM

SERVES 8

16 slices grilled sourdough
  bread (see page 96)

8 garlic cloves, peeled

3/4 to 1 lb [340 to 455 g]
  very ripe medium
  tomatoes (2 or 3), halved
  crosswise

Kosher salt and freshly
  ground black pepper

Extra-virgin olive oil, for
  drizzling

16 slices Serrano ham

Tomato toasts, or *pan con tomate,* are a specialty of the Catalan region of Spain. This recipe requires nothing more than a few very ripe tomatoes, garlic, olive oil, and grilled bread. It's fantastic on its own or with a slice of Serrano ham and goes brilliantly with Spanish Cava or manzanilla sherry.

Arrange the bread slices on a work surface. Rub them with garlic, then with the halved tomatoes until the juice of the tomatoes is absorbed and the surface of the bread is red and juicy. Discard the garlic and tomatoes. Sprinkle each toast generously with salt and pepper and drizzle with olive oil.

Top each bread slice with a piece of Serrano ham and serve.

MAKE AHEAD: The toasts can be prepared about 1 hour ahead of time. Drizzle with olive oil and top with the ham just before serving.

CHAPTER 6

SEAFOOD

Fresh fish and shellfish dishes add a layer of sophisticated flavor to any type of spread. From chilled shrimp to clams and mussels on the half shell to a gorgeous whole poached salmon, savory, scrumptious bites from the sea are a welcome addition to any table. .

PICKLED SHRIMP

SERVES 6 TO 8

PICKLED SHRIMP:

Kosher salt

2 lb [910 g] shell-on large
shrimp

4 garlic cloves, thinly sliced

1 medium white or red
onion, thinly sliced

½ medium fennel bulb,
thinly sliced

½ jalapeño pepper, seeded
and thinly sliced

¼ cup [60 ml] white wine
vinegar

¼ cup [60 ml] extra-virgin
olive oil

2 Tbsp fresh lemon juice

1 Tbsp lemon zest

Freshly ground black
pepper

continued

Served with spicy remoulade sauce and fresh lemon
wedges, pickled shrimp is always the star of the table.
This dish is very easy to prepare and tastes great after
marinating and chilling in the refrigerator for a few
hours or even a day. Crisp Sauvignon Blanc or dry rosé
would be good wine choices for this shrimp recipe.

To make the pickled shrimp: Bring a large pot of
salted water to a boil, add the shrimp, and cook
until just opaque in the center, 2 to 3 minutes.
Drain and rinse under cold running water to cool.
Peel and devein, leaving the tails intact.

In a large nonreactive bowl, combine the shrimp,
garlic, onion, fennel, jalapeño, vinegar, oil, lemon
juice, and lemon zest. Season with salt and pepper
and toss to combine. Cover and refrigerate, stirring
occasionally, for at least 4 hours or up to overnight.

continued

RED REMOULADE SAUCE:

1 celery stalk, finely chopped

1 cup [240 g] mayonnaise

¼ cup [65 g] ketchup

2 Tbsp Dijon mustard

2 Tbsp horseradish

1 Tbsp celery salt

1 Tbsp hot sauce

Kosher salt

Lemon wedges, for serving

To make the red remoulade sauce: In a medium bowl, whisk together the celery, mayonnaise, ketchup, mustard, horseradish, celery salt, and hot sauce until well combined. Season with salt. (See Make Ahead.)

Remove the shrimp from the pickling mixture and arrange them on a platter. Serve with the remoulade sauce and lemon wedges.

MAKE AHEAD: The shrimp will keep, tightly covered in the refrigerator, for up to 4 hours or overnight. The sauce will keep, tightly covered in the refrigerator, for up to 3 days. Taste and adjust the seasoning, if necessary, before serving.

ROASTED SHRIMP COCKTAIL

SERVES 6 TO 8

¼ cup [60 ml] extra-virgin olive oil

¼ cup [60 ml] fresh lime juice

2 Tbsp soy sauce

1 Tbsp honey

1 Tbsp sriracha

2 garlic cloves, minced

2 lb [910 g] large shrimp, peeled and deveined, tails left on

Lime wedges, for serving

Served hot or cold, this shrimp dish is quite delicious and has a good kick of heat from sriracha sauce. A Spanish white Rioja or Falanghina from southern Italy works well with these rich and spicy shrimp.

In a large nonreactive bowl, whisk together the olive oil, lime juice, soy sauce, honey, sriracha, and garlic until combined. Add the shrimp and stir until well coated with the marinade. Cover and refrigerate for 1 to 2 hours.

Preheat the oven to 400°F [200°C].

Using a slotted spoon, transfer the shrimp to a baking sheet and roast for 8 to 10 minutes, until the shrimp are firm and cooked through. Let cool (see Make Ahead).

Arrange the shrimp on a serving platter, garnish with lime wedges, and serve.

MAKE AHEAD: These are also very good served cold. The shrimp can be stored, tightly covered in the refrigerator, for up to 1 day before serving.

MUSSELS WITH CHORIZO & BREAD CRUMBS

SERVES 6 TO 8

½ cup [120 ml] dry white wine

2 lb [910 g] (about 3 dozen) mussels, scrubbed, rinsed, and debearded (see Note)

3 Tbsp unsalted butter

3 oz [85 g] chorizo, casing removed, minced

2 tsp finely minced garlic

¾ cup [45 g] panko

3 Tbsp chopped fresh flat-leaf parsley

Kosher salt and freshly ground black pepper

Extra-virgin olive oil, for drizzling

Lemon wedges, for serving

Mussels are a marvelous, versatile, and inexpensive appetizer that you will want to serve often. Here they are cooked until they open and served in their shells with a savory chorizo-and-panko topping after a quick broil in the oven. Pair them with a Chenin Blanc or an unoaked Chardonnay.

Pour the wine into a large pot with a lid and bring to a boil over high heat. Add the mussels, lower the heat to medium-low, cover, and cook until the mussels open, 6 to 8 minutes. Using a slotted spoon, transfer the mussels to a large bowl. Discard any unopened or broken mussels. Strain the cooking liquid and reserve. When cool enough to handle, remove the mussels from their shells and transfer them to a bowl. Reserve half of the mussel shells (you'll need 36 half shells).

Melt the butter in a large skillet over medium heat. Add the chorizo and garlic and cook until lightly browned, about 3 minutes. Lower the heat to low, add the panko and parsley, season with salt and pepper, and cook, stirring, until well blended, about 5 minutes. Add a bit of the reserved cooking liquid if the mixture seems too dry. Remove from the heat (see Make Ahead).

Preheat the broiler. Spoon the mussels into the reserved shells and top each with some of the panko mixture. Arrange the filled shells on a large rimmed baking sheet and drizzle with olive oil. Broil until the topping is sizzling and lightly browned, 3 to 5 minutes. Transfer the mussels to a platter and serve with lemon wedges.

MAKE AHEAD: The panko mixture can be made a few hours ahead of time, covered, and kept at room temperature.

NOTE: When buying mussels, purchase the freshest ones available. Scrub the shells, rinse in a few changes of cold water, and remove the beards just before cooking. If they are removed too far ahead of time, the mussels will be inedible.

MUSSELS WITH SALSA

SERVES 6 TO 8

3 ripe plum tomatoes, finely chopped

1 jalapeño pepper, seeded and minced

½ red onion, finely chopped

2 Tbsp chopped fresh cilantro

1 Tbsp fresh lime juice

1 tsp balsamic vinegar

Kosher salt and freshly ground black pepper

2 shallots, chopped

2 garlic cloves, thinly sliced

½ cup [120 ml] dry white wine

2 lb [910 g] (about 3 dozen) mussels, scrubbed, rinsed, and debearded (see Note, page 117)

Lime wedges, for serving

A platter of bright and beautiful chilled mussels topped with fresh tomatoes and herbs is just the right thing to serve at a summertime get-together. They are delectable with a white wine such as Albariño or a dry Riesling.

In a large bowl, combine the tomatoes, jalapeño, onion, cilantro, lime juice, and vinegar, season with salt and pepper, and set aside.

Place the shallots, garlic, and wine in a large pot with a lid and bring to a boil over high heat. Add the mussels, lower the heat to medium-low, cover, and cook until the mussels open, 6 to 8 minutes. Using a slotted spoon, transfer the mussels to a large bowl. Discard any unopened or broken mussels. Strain the cooking liquid and reserve. When cool enough to handle, remove the mussels from their shells and transfer them to a bowl. Reserve half of the mussel shells (you'll need 36 half shells).

Add about 2 tablespoons of the reserved cooking liquid to the salsa and stir. Add the mussels to the bowl, toss everything together, cover, and refrigerate for at least 2 hours.

To serve, spoon the mussels and salsa into the mussel shells and spoon a bit of the remaining salsa over them. Transfer to a serving platter, if desired, and serve with lime wedges. This dish doesn't keep well and is best enjoyed within 2 hours of making; keep the mussels refrigerated during that time.

BAKED CLAMS WITH PESTO

SERVES 6 TO 8

24 littleneck clams, scrubbed and rinsed

1 cup [12 g] packed fresh basil leaves

¼ cup [30 g] pine nuts or walnuts

2 Tbsp chopped fresh flat-leaf parsley

2 Tbsp chopped fresh chives

1 Tbsp chopped fresh tarragon

1 large garlic clove

¼ cup [60 ml] extra-virgin olive oil

¼ cup [8 g] freshly grated Parmesan cheese

Kosher salt and freshly ground black pepper

¼ cup [10 g] fine fresh bread crumbs

Hot sauce, for serving

Lemon wedges, for serving

Clams on the half shell are fantastic, but opening them can be very time consuming for a busy host. Happily, they will open on their own after a few minutes in the oven. For a twist on classic baked clams, top them with fresh pesto sauce and bread crumbs and bake until they just begin to sizzle. You can't go wrong serving these succulent, briny treats along with a few bottles of Albariño.

Preheat the oven to 450°F [230°C].

Place the clams on a rimmed baking sheet and bake until they open, 10 to 12 minutes. When cool enough to handle, remove the upper shells and return the clams on the half shell to the baking sheet.

Meanwhile, combine the basil, pine nuts, parsley, chives, tarragon, and garlic in a food processor and pulse until minced. With the machine on, slowly pour in the oil until smooth and emulsified (see Make Ahead). Transfer the mixture to a medium bowl. Add the Parmesan and season with salt and pepper, adding a bit more oil, if needed; stir to combine.

Spoon a bit of pesto over each clam and sprinkle with the bread crumbs. Bake until the topping is lightly browned and sizzling, about 5 minutes. Arrange the clams on a platter and serve at once with hot sauce and lemon wedges.

MAKE AHEAD: The pesto can be prepared, up to the point prior to adding the Parmesan, a day ahead of time. Bring to room temperature and add the cheese and salt and pepper before adding to the clams.

ROASTED OYSTERS

SERVES 6 TO 8

24 medium oysters

6 thick slices country bread

Unsalted butter or extra-virgin olive oil, for brushing

Juice of ½ orange

Extra-virgin olive oil, for drizzling

Sea salt and freshly ground black pepper

1 cup [20 to 40 g] chopped mixed fresh herbs, such as flat-leaf parsley, basil, cilantro, and mint

Oysters can also be cooked without shucking—they will pop open after about 10 minutes of roasting in the oven. In this elegant dish, the oysters are finished with orange, olive oil, and fresh herbs. There are many tried-and-true wine pairings for oysters; among them are Muscadet, dry fino sherry, and, of course, Champagne.

Preheat the oven to 375°F [190°C].

Arrange the oysters, rounded-side down, on a baking sheet. Roast until the oysters start to pop open, about 10 minutes. Meanwhile, grill or toast the bread and brush with butter (see page 96 for instructions on grilling bread). Remove the oysters from the oven, let them cool a bit and, with an oyster knife or other small sharp knife, carefully remove the top shells from each one. Detach the oysters from the bottom shells, keeping the liquid in the shells.

Arrange the oysters on a platter or individual plates. Drizzle them with the orange juice and olive oil, season with sea salt and pepper, and garnish with the herbs. Serve with the toast.

TUNA CRUDO

SERVES 6 TO 8

1 lb [455 g] sushi-grade yellowfin tuna

¼ cup [60 ml] extra-virgin olive oil

2 Tbsp fresh lemon juice

1 medium shallot, finely diced

2 tsp drained capers

1 tsp lemon zest

½ red chile pepper, seeded and thinly sliced, or ¼ tsp red pepper flakes

Kosher salt and freshly ground black pepper

Chopped fresh basil or chives, for garnish

"Sushi-quality" or "sushi-grade" tuna is the key ingredient in this elegant crudo (Italian for "raw"). When buying it, look for the best and freshest you can find—it may cost more than regular tuna, but the results are well worth it. Freeze the tuna for easier slicing and serve it with crunchy rice crackers and fresh cucumber rounds. Choosing a wine to drink with sushi-style dishes can be tricky, but this is wonderful with sake or an aromatic Torrentés.

Place the tuna in the freezer for 10 minutes. Using a very sharp knife, cut the tuna into 1/8 inch [4 mm] slices. Arrange them in a single layer on a serving platter (see Make Ahead).

In a small bowl, whisk together the olive oil and lemon juice. Add the shallot, capers, lemon zest, and chile pepper and whisk again. Drizzle the vinaigrette over the tuna, season with salt and pepper, garnish with basil, and serve.

MAKE AHEAD: The tuna can be prepared up to 3 hours ahead of time; cover the platter with plastic wrap and refrigerate until ready to dress and serve.

FISH & SCALLOP CEVICHE

SERVES 6 TO 8

1 lb [455 g] skinless fish fillets, such as snapper, bass, or halibut, diced into ½ in [12 mm] pieces

8 oz [230 g] sea scallops, cut into small pieces

½ cup [120 ml] fresh lime juice

¼ cup [60 ml] fresh lemon juice

½ cup [60 g] seeded and diced red bell pepper

½ cup [60 g] seeded and diced yellow bell pepper

3 green onions (white and green parts), thinly sliced

1 small jalapeño pepper, stemmed, seeded, and diced

1 garlic clove, minced

¼ cup [60 ml] extra-virgin olive oil

Pinch of sugar

Dash of hot sauce

Kosher salt and freshly ground black pepper

Cool and refreshing ceviche is a perfect party food because it's easy to prepare and can be marinated well ahead of time. In this recipe, mild fish fillets and sea scallops "cook" in lime and lemon juices and are then tossed together with a mélange of peppers and green onions. This version of ceviche is delicious with Sauvignon Blanc or Muscadet.

In a large nonreactive bowl, toss the fish, scallops, lime juice, and lemon juice together. Cover and refrigerate for 1½ hours, stirring occasionally (see Make Ahead). Strain the mixture from the juice and transfer to a clean bowl. Discard the citrus juice.

Place the bell peppers, green onions, jalapeño, and garlic in a medium bowl. In a small bowl, whisk together the olive oil, sugar, and hot sauce and then stir it into the bell pepper mixture. Season with salt and black pepper. Add the bell pepper mixture to the fish mixture and gently toss together (see Make Ahead).

½ cup [20 g] chopped
fresh cilantro

Tortilla chips or grilled
bread (see page 96),
for serving

Stir the cilantro into the ceviche and serve with
tortilla chips or grilled bread.

MAKE AHEAD: The fish can be marinated and
completely drained on the day you're going to
serve it; cover tightly and refrigerate for up to
6 hours. Add the bell pepper mixture and season
the ceviche within 2 hours of serving; keep it
refrigerated until ready to serve.

RED SNAPPER, CRAB & SQUID CEVICHE

SERVES 6 TO 8

8 oz [230 g] red snapper fillet, skinned and cut into ¼ in [6 mm] cubes

8 oz [230 g] crabmeat

8 oz [230 g] squid, cut into rings

1½ cups [360 ml] fresh lime juice

½ cup [60 g] diced red bell pepper

½ cup [60 g] diced yellow bell pepper

1 jalapeño pepper, seeded, deveined, and minced

½ cup [80 g] diced plum tomatoes

¼ cup [60 ml] extra-virgin olive oil

Kosher salt and freshly ground black pepper

1 avocado, halved, pitted, peeled, and diced

1 small red onion, finely chopped

2 Tbsp chopped fresh cilantro

Tortilla chips or grilled bread (see page 96), for serving

Red snapper has a mild flavor and delicate taste that plays well with other fish; it works beautifully with crabmeat and rings of fresh squid in this ceviche. When preparing any raw fish dishes, always use the freshest and highest-quality seafood available. This light and summery appetizer is lovely served with either White Wine, Orange & Mint Sangria (page 181), or Rosé & Peach Sangria (page 183).

In a large nonreactive bowl, toss the red snapper, crabmeat, squid, and lime juice together. Cover and refrigerate the mixture, stirring occasionally, for at least 5 hours or until the fish has lost its transparency and become opaque.

About 1 hour before serving, add the bell peppers, jalapeño, tomatoes, and olive oil and toss together. Season with salt and pepper and refrigerate for at least another hour.

Remove from the refrigerator and drain the excess juice. Add the avocado, onion, and cilantro, gently toss together, and serve with tortilla chips or grilled bread.

MAKE AHEAD: The ceviche can be made up to 6 hours ahead of time.

BUYING SEAFOOD

Buying fresh seafood can be daunting, so it's best to find a reliable seafood counter or store and get to know the fishmonger and the store's suppliers. When in doubt, ask. Here are some buying tips:

Fish
* The best smell is no smell. Raw fish should smell fresh and mild, not "fishy."
* Whole fish should have firm skin, bright-colored gills, and clear eyes.
* Look for fish fillets that have a bright, uniform color across their surfaces. Discoloring or dark spots indicate that the fillets aren't fresh.

Clams, Oysters & Mussels
* Bivalves should smell briny and sweet, like seaweed, not "fishy" at all.
* Shells should be tightly closed with no cracks or chips.

Scallops
* Flesh should be translucent and firm with a white coat.
* Avoid any scallops that smell "fishy" or like iodine.

Shrimp
* Fresh shrimp are highly perishable, so choose wisely. Pass on any that smell like ammonia or have black spots. These are signs that the shrimp are not fresh.

WHOLE POACHED SALMON

SERVES 8 TO 10

One 3 lb [1.4 kg] whole skin-on salmon fillet

Kosher salt and freshly ground black pepper

1 cup [240 ml] white wine

1 yellow onion, sliced

½ tsp peppercorns

8 sprigs fresh flat-leaf parsley

8 sprigs dill, plus more for garnish

2 cucumbers, thinly sliced, for garnish

Fresh lemon wedges, for garnish

Sauces of your choice, for serving

More than a bite, a beautiful, whole poached salmon, garnished with cucumbers and fresh dill, is a show-stopper. It's great to serve with a variety of sauces, such as Avocado Cream (page 52), Watercress Sauce (page 106), or Tzatziki (page 161). Salmon pairs well with many white wines, and a good one to try here is an Italian Vermentino. A chilled Pinot Noir or dry rosé would taste great with it too.

Pat the salmon dry with paper towels and season with salt and pepper. Place 1 cup [240 ml] of water, the wine, onion, peppercorns, parsley, and dill into a roasting pan or fish poacher large enough to hold the fillet. Add the salmon. If it's not covered by liquid, add just enough water to barely cover the fillet and gently bring to a simmer over medium-low heat. Cover and simmer for about 10 minutes, until the salmon is just opaque in the center.

Remove the pan from the heat and let the salmon cool slightly in the liquid. Using two spatulas, transfer the salmon to a large platter. Using a paper towel, dab off any white bits and let stand at room temperature for 15 minutes. Cover loosely with plastic wrap and refrigerate for several hours.

Using a sharp knife, peel the skin off the salmon. Garnish the platter with fresh dill, sliced cucumbers, and lemon wedges. Serve with desired sauces.

MAKE AHEAD: The salmon will keep, loosely covered in the refrigerator, for up to 8 hours before serving.

CHAPTER 7
MEAT

These hearty bites—chicken and sausages hot off the grill, scrumptious brisket sliders, and platters of charcuterie—are sure to please your guests and whet their appetites for more wine. They pair well with a variety of wines that complement their rich and salty flavors.

SPICY GRILLED CHICKEN BITES

SERVES 6 TO 8

½ cup [100 g] light brown sugar

¼ cup [60 ml] rice vinegar

¼ cup [60 ml] nam pla (fish sauce)

1 Tbsp hot chile paste (such as Sambal Oelek)

2 tsp finely grated peeled ginger

3 lb [1.4 kg] skinless, boneless chicken thighs

The marinade for this grilled chicken is loaded with sweet, hot, and funky flavors and makes a superb warm dipping sauce. Good wines to drink with these tasty bites include white Côtes du Rhône or Riesling, red Malbec or Zinfandel, or a chilled rosé.

In a large bowl, whisk together the sugar, vinegar, fish sauce, chile paste, and ginger. Add the chicken and toss to coat. Cover and let the chicken marinate in the refrigerator for 1 hour.

Prepare a charcoal or gas grill for high heat. Remove the chicken from the marinade, reserving the marinade. Grill the chicken, turning once, until cooked through, about 6 minutes. Remove from the heat and tent the chicken with aluminum foil, 5 to 10 minutes. Transfer the reserved marinade to a small saucepan. Bring to a boil over medium-high heat, lower the heat to low, and simmer for about 5 minutes.

Cut the chicken into bite-size pieces and serve with short skewers or toothpicks and the warm marinade on the side.

NOTE: The marinade will keep, tightly covered in the refrigerator, for up to 3 days.

GRILLED SAUSAGE BITES
WITH TARRAGON-MUSTARD SAUCE

SERVES 6 TO 8

TARRAGON-MUSTARD
SAUCE:

¹/₄ cup [60 g] Dijon mustard

2 Tbsp rice wine vinegar

2 Tbsp chopped fresh
tarragon leaves

Freshly ground black
pepper

3 lb [1.4 kg] hot and sweet
Italian sausages

With so many varieties of good sausage available in specialty markets and butcher shops, you can pick and choose your favorites. They may be hot, spicy, mild, or sweet. In this recipe, I use a combination of sweet and hot Italian sausage because they both go so well with mustard sauce, but really almost any type will work well on the grill. Grilled sausage tastes great with Pinot Blanc and Riesling, and it also pairs well with a peppery Syrah from California.

To make the tarragon-mustard sauce: In a bowl, stir together the mustard, vinegar, tarragon, and pepper (see Make Ahead).

Prepare a gas or charcoal grill for high heat. Grill the sausages for 8 to 10 minutes, turning once or twice, until cooked through and lightly charred.

Cut the sausages into bite-size pieces and serve on toothpicks with the tarragon-mustard sauce.

MAKE AHEAD: The sauce will keep, tightly covered in the refrigerator, for up to 3 days.

GRILLED HANGER STEAK

SERVES 8

Two 1½ lb [680 g] hanger
steaks, trimmed,
membrane removed
(see Note)

Extra-virgin olive oil, for
brushing and drizzling

Kosher salt and freshly
ground black pepper

4 cups [80 g] fresh arugula
leaves, for serving

Grilled bread (see page
96), for serving

Chimichurri Sauce (page
155), for serving (optional)

Hanger steak, also known as butcher's steak, has a rich
and meaty flavor and is a good, inexpensive alternative
to pricier cuts of beef. Look for it at butcher shops
and buy it trimmed with its membrane removed. For
the best results, grill the steak quickly over fairly hot
heat and serve it thinly sliced with grilled bread and
Chimichurri Sauce (page 155). There are a number of
excellent wines to drink with this: robust red Bordeaux,
Malbec, or domestic Pinot Noir, to name just a few.

Brush the steaks with olive oil and season generously
with salt and pepper. Cover and let stand at room
temperature for 30 minutes.

Prepare a charcoal or gas grill for medium-high
heat. Grill the steaks for 5 to 6 minutes on each side
(for medium-rare). Transfer the steaks to a cutting
board and let rest for 10 minutes. Slice the steaks
across the grain into thin pieces.

Arrange the arugula on a large platter, top with the
steak, and drizzle with a bit of olive oil. Serve with
grilled bread and chimichurri sauce (if desired).
This dish doesn't keep well and is best enjoyed the
day it's made.

NOTE: If you cannot find hanger steak, flank steak is
a good substitution.

BRISKET SLIDERS

SERVES 12

MARINADE AND BRISKET:

2 cups [480 ml] red wine

¼ cup [60 ml] red wine
vinegar

2 carrots, coarsely chopped

2 garlic cloves, thinly sliced

1 celery stalk, coarsely
chopped

1 large white onion,
coarsely chopped, plus
2 large white onions,
finely chopped

2½ lb [1.2 kg] beef brisket,
fat trimmed

Kosher salt and freshly
ground black pepper

¼ cup [60 ml] vegetable oil

1 Tbsp tomato paste

1 tsp paprika

1 bay leaf

1 Tbsp chopped thyme
leaves

½ cup [120 ml] chicken
broth

Brisket is so rich and luscious, it's hard to believe
that it's so easy to make. All you need are a few basic
ingredients and the time to marinate and braise it.
Slider rolls filled with tasty slices of brisket, horseradish
mustard, and pickled red onions make perfect sandwiches for a gathering. Full-flavored Merlot or Shiraz
pair well with these hearty bites.

To make the marinade and brisket: Combine the
wine, vinegar, carrots, garlic, celery, and coarsely
chopped onion in a medium bowl. Transfer to a
large, resealable plastic bag and add the brisket.
Close the bag, pressing out any air, and refrigerate
the brisket overnight or for up to 2 days. (Alternatively, transfer the marinade and the brisket to
a large nonreactive dish, cover, and let marinate
in the refrigerator.)

Preheat the oven to 275°F [140°C].

Strain the marinade into a bowl and discard the
solids. Pat the brisket dry with paper towels and
season generously with salt and pepper. Heat the
oil in a large Dutch oven with a lid over medium
heat, add the brisket, and cook, turning once, until
browned on both sides, 8 to 10 minutes.

HORSERADISH MUSTARD:

½ cup [120 g] Dijon
  mustard

1 Tbsp prepared
  horseradish

12 mini brioche or
  hamburger slider rolls,
  split, for serving

Pickled Red Onions
  (page 90, optional)

Transfer the brisket to a plate. Add the finely chopped onions to the Dutch oven and cook over medium heat until softened, about 5 minutes. Add the tomato paste and paprika and cook, stirring, for 2 minutes. Return the brisket to the Dutch oven and add the bay leaf, thyme, and reserved marinade. Add salt and pepper and bring to a simmer. Cover and braise in the oven for about 3 hours, until the meat is very tender, turning the brisket halfway through cooking.

Transfer the brisket to a plate; cover and keep warm. Add any cooking juices from the plate and the broth to the Dutch oven and bring to a boil over high heat, scraping up any brown bits in the bottom of the pan. Cook, stirring occasionally, until the sauce is thickened and reduced by half, about 10 minutes.

To make the horseradish mustard: In a small bowl, whisk together the Dijon mustard and horseradish until combined.

Slice the brisket into thin slices across the grain. Arrange the meat on the slider rolls, top with a bit of the reduced brisket sauce, a dollop of horseradish mustard, and pickled onions (if desired), and serve.

MAKE AHEAD: The brisket and sauce will keep, tightly covered in the refrigerator, for up to 2 days. Reheat the brisket in the oven before serving.

BISCUITS & DEVILED HAM

MAKES 12 BISCUIT SANDWICHES

BISCUITS:

2 cups [280 g] unbleached all-purpose flour, plus more for dusting

2 Tbsp baking powder

1 Tbsp sugar

½ tsp kosher salt

7 Tbsp [100 g] cold unsalted butter

¾ cup [180 ml] whole milk

Homemade biscuits are always a tasty treat. Here they're served with a flavor-packed deviled ham spread that can be made with leftover baked ham or cooked ham from the deli. The spread is also terrific to spoon onto crackers or cucumber rounds, or to stuff into celery stalks or endive leaves. These elegant little biscuit bites taste great with Muscadet, Pinot Blanc, or rosé.

To make the biscuits: Position an oven rack in the center of the oven and preheat the oven to 450°F [230°C].

Whisk together the flour, baking powder, sugar, and salt in a large mixing bowl. Transfer to a food processor, cut the butter into pats, and add to the flour mixture, then pulse five or six times until the mixture resembles rough crumbs. Add the milk and blend until the dough just comes together. (Alternatively, cut the butter into the flour mixture in the bowl using a pastry cutter or two knives. Add the milk and stir with a fork until the dough forms a rough ball.)

Turn the dough out onto a well-floured surface and roll the dough to a ¾ inch [2 cm] thickness with a floured rolling pin. Using a 2½ inch [6 cm] biscuit cutter or a small juice or wineglass, cut out as many rounds as you can. Press the scraps together, roll out again, and cut out more biscuits. Transfer the rounds to a baking sheet and bake the biscuits until golden, about 12 minutes. Let cool on a wire rack.

DEVILED HAM:

8 oz [230 g] cooked ham
(not sliced), coarsely
chopped

Heaping ⅓ cup [85 g]
cream cheese, at room
temperature

¼ cup [60 g] mayonnaise

2 tsp whole-grain mustard

1 tsp hot sauce

1 tsp sweet pickle relish

1 tsp fresh lemon juice

2 green onions (white
and green parts), finely
chopped

2 Tbsp finely chopped
fresh flat-leaf parsley

Freshly ground black
pepper

Watercress sprigs,
stemmed, or arugula
leaves, for serving

To make the deviled ham: Place the ham, cream cheese, mayonnaise, mustard, hot sauce, relish, and lemon juice in a food processor and pulse until fairly smooth, scraping down the sides of the bowl as necessary.

Transfer the mixture to a medium bowl, add the green onions and parsley, season with pepper, and mix well. Cover and refrigerate for at least 1 hour before serving.

Split the biscuits in half crosswise, spread a generous amount of the ham mixture onto the bottom halves of the biscuits, top with watercress, cover with the biscuit tops, and serve.

MAKE AHEAD: The deviled ham will keep, tightly covered in the refrigerator, for up to 2 days. Taste and adjust the seasoning, if necessary, before serving.

PORK & RICOTTA MEATBALLS

SERVES 8 TO 10

1/3 cup [20 g] panko

1/4 cup [60 ml] whole milk

1 lb [455 g] ground
(minced) pork

4 oz [115 g] whole-milk
ricotta cheese

1/4 cup [8 g] freshly grated
Parmesan cheese

1 large egg, lightly beaten

1 tsp fines herbes or herbes
de Provençe

Pinch of freshly grated
nutmeg

Kosher salt and freshly
ground black pepper

Extra-virgin olive oil, for
brushing

Chopped fresh flat-leaf
parsley, for garnish

Marinara (page 159), for
serving (optional)

Meatballs are always very popular at gatherings and it seems like nobody can eat just one. Ricotta cheese is the key ingredient in this recipe because it makes the meatballs quite tender. They're very good to serve with Marinara (page 159) for dipping, or as sliders (see Note). Chianti Classico and full-bodied Zinfandel always complement red meat, and either one would be a good choice to serve here.

In a large mixing bowl, mix together the panko and the milk and let stand for 5 minutes. Add the pork, cheeses, egg, herbs, and nutmeg. Season with salt and pepper and work the mixture together with your hands until it is well incorporated.

Form the mixture into thirty balls that are 1 inch [2.5 cm] in diameter and arrange them on a baking sheet lined with parchment paper. Cover and refrigerate until well chilled, up to 2 hours or overnight.

Position an oven rack in the center of the oven and preheat the oven to 425°F [220°C].

Brush the meatballs with olive oil and bake until golden and cooked through, turning once halfway through baking, about 12 minutes total. Transfer to a platter, garnish with parsley, and serve with marinara sauce (if desired).

continued

MAKE AHEAD: The meatballs can be prepared and refrigerated up to 1 day ahead of time. They can also be baked and then stored in the freezer for up to 1 month. Thaw and bake them for about 25 minutes in a 425°F [220°F] oven.

NOTE: For delicious mini-meatball sandwiches, or sliders, heat the meatballs in a large saucepan over medium heat with enough tomato sauce to cover. Once warm, spoon the meatballs into mini-hamburger or slider rolls. Sprinkle with freshly grated Parmesan cheese, garnish with parsley, and serve.

LAMB MEATBALLS

SERVES 8

1¼ lb [570 g] ground lamb, chilled (see Note)

1 large egg, beaten

¼ cup [35 g] dry bread crumbs

¼ red onion, finely chopped

1 garlic clove, finely chopped

1 Tbsp finely chopped fresh cilantro

1 Tbsp finely chopped mint

½ tsp ground cumin

¼ tsp ground cinnamon

Kosher salt and freshly ground black pepper

Fresh lemon juice, for sprinkling

Juicy and beautifully spiced with cumin and cinnamon, lamb meatballs are lovely to serve with Tzatziki (page 161) or Herbed Yogurt Dip (page 32) and warm pita bread. Fruity reds like Tempranillo and Cabernet Sauvignon pair very well with lamb.

Position an oven rack in the center of the oven and preheat the oven to 375°F [190°C]. Line a baking sheet with parchment paper.

In a large mixing bowl, combine the lamb, egg, bread crumbs, onion, garlic, cilantro, mint, cumin, and cinnamon; season with salt and pepper; and mix thoroughly using your hands. Form the mixture into thirty balls that are 1 inch [2.5 cm] in diameter and arrange them on the prepared baking sheet. Bake the meatballs until lightly browned, 12 to 15 minutes, turning once halfway through baking.

Sprinkle the meatballs with a bit of fresh lemon juice and serve with toothpicks or small serving forks and Tzatziki or Herbed Yogurt Dip on the side.

MAKE AHEAD: The meatballs can be prepared and refrigerated for up to 1 day. They can also be baked, then stored in the freezer for up to 1 month. Thaw and bake them in a 375°F [190°C] oven for about 15 minutes.

NOTE: The lamb is easier to combine and roll when it is chilled.

CHARCUTERIE

Charcuterie comes from the French *chair* ("flesh") and *cuit* ("cooked") and it describes a wide range of cured meats in which pork plays a big role.

Creating a sumptuous charcuterie board loaded with cured meats, pâtés, and terrines accompanied by an assortment of cheeses, nuts, tangy pickles, olives, mustards, sweet jams and preserves, dried and fresh fruit, and a few loaves of crusty bread is always a crowd-pleaser. It's an easy and rewarding way to satisfy your hungriest guests. In addition, charcuterie and its accoutrements are full of rich, salty, and nutty flavors and textures that perfectly complement wine.

SHOPPING

For busy hosts who don't have the time to cook or who prefer not to, a charcuterie board is the ideal wine bite to serve, and it's a breeze to put together. Look for ingredients at gourmet shops, delicatessens, and local Italian or other ethnic specialty shops. To figure out how much meat to buy, here's a good rule of thumb: If you're serving charcuterie as part of a larger buffet or spread, estimate about 2 ounces [55 g] per person. If it's the main course, estimate about 5 ounces [140 g] per person.

When shopping for charcuterie, buy a wide variety of meats. The basic categories are *crudo* (raw cured meat) and *cotto* (cooked meat). Cured meats, such as prosciutto and salami, are saltier and more intense and should be balanced with the fattiness and sweetness of cooked meats, such as ham and mortadella, as well as spreadable pâtés and terrines. Be sure to buy your ingredients as close to party time as possible, so flavors are at their best. Store meats in the refrigerator and handle them while they are well chilled; the slices are easier to work with. Charcuterie should be served at room temperature.

WHAT TO SERVE: PRE-SLICED, UNSLICED, AND SPREADABLE

Some excellent examples of pre-sliced meats include prosciutto, bresaola, guanciale, mortadella, and speck. Serve them flat or in loose rolls, thinly sliced and overlapping, so your guests can easily serve themselves.

Good types of unsliced meats include hard salami, soppressata, saucisson sec, smoked sausage or ham, finocchiona, and capicola. Serve these on a cutting board and cut several rounds when you set the board out so your guests will be encouraged to slice more and serve themselves.

Other important components to include on the charcuterie board are spreadable preparations, such as rich and rustic pâtés, rillettes, and terrines.

ACCENTS

Any number of tasty and beautiful accoutrements can be added to the board. Make sure they vary in texture, color, and flavor. Good accompaniments include cheese; olives; pickles and pickled vegetables (pages 88–92); assorted nuts; dried fruit; jam, preserves, and chutneys (pages 164–69); mustard; crackers; breads and breadsticks; and very fresh fruit, such as apples, grapes, melon, and berries.

WINE

There are a number of wines that pair well with charcuterie. You can't go wrong with almost any wine, but some stand-out selections include hearty reds like Merlot or Malbec or lighter-but-earthy Pinot Noir to complement the tastes of the meat. Champagne or sparkling wines, such as Prosecco or Cava, are good choices too, and brighter white wines, such as Pinot Gris and Albariño, cut the rich and salty flavors of charcuterie beautifully.

MAKE AHEAD

You can prepare the board a few hours in advance and store it, lightly covered with plastic wrap, in the refrigerator. Remove the board an hour before serving and add any accompaniments just before serving.

CHAPTER 8

SAUCES & CONDIMENTS

A good sauce or condiment adds the perfect finishing touch to any type of dish. These recipes are excellent accompaniments to a number of other dishes in this book. They can be made in a matter of minutes with fresh ingredients and taste much better than store-bought versions.

GREMOLATA

MAKES ABOUT 1¼ CUPS [65 G]

1¼ cups [50 g] fresh flat-leaf parsley, rinsed and dried

2 garlic cloves

Zest of ½ lemon

Pinch of kosher salt

Gremolata is a simple garnish that is often served with lamb and osso buco. It adds a nice, bright finishing touch to other dishes like deviled eggs, bruschetta, and Lamb Meatballs (page 145). When preparing it, be sure to use very fresh flat-leaf parsley that has been thoroughly rinsed and dried. The brightness of this sauce is offset nicely by a Cabernet Sauvignon or Malbec.

Using a very sharp knife, finely chop the parsley and thinly slice the garlic. Add the lemon zest and continue to chop until the parsley, garlic, and zest are well combined. If the mixture seems too damp, spread it on a baking sheet for 1 hour to dry at room temperature. Add a pinch of salt before serving.

MAKE AHEAD: Gremolata is best enjoyed the day it is made but it will keep, covered in the refrigerator, for up to 1 day.

CHIMICHURRI SAUCE

¼ cup [10 g] coarsely chopped fresh flat-leaf parsley

¼ cup [10 g] coarsely chopped fresh cilantro

4 large garlic cloves, minced

3 Tbsp red wine vinegar

2 Tbsp chopped fresh oregano

1 tsp red pepper flakes

Kosher salt and freshly ground pepper

½ cup [120 ml] extra-virgin olive oil

Chimichurri is a garlicky green sauce that is typically served with grilled steak (page 135) and other meats. It's a natural pairing with red Rioja and Pinot Noir.

Place the parsley, cilantro, garlic, vinegar, oregano, and red pepper flakes in a food processor and blend until smooth. Season with salt and pepper. Transfer the sauce to a bowl, pour the olive oil over the mixture, and gently stir. Let the sauce stand for at least 20 minutes before serving.

MAKE AHEAD: The chimichurri will keep, tightly covered in the refrigerator, for 1 week. Bring to room temperature and stir well before serving.

TOMATILLO SAUCE

MAKES ABOUT 2 CUPS [450 G]

1 lb [455 g] tomatillos, husked, rinsed, and halved or quartered, depending on the size

1 white onion, peeled and quartered

1 large jalapeño pepper, seeded and minced (see Note)

2 garlic cloves, thinly sliced

½ cup [20 g] chopped fresh cilantro

2 Tbsp fresh lime juice

Kosher salt and freshly ground black pepper

Tomatillo sauce is a very important element in Mexican cooking—it's a savory complement to tortilla chips, tacos, quesadillas, and many meat, fish, and egg dishes. Small, pale-green tomatillos have the same growing season as red ones and are available at supermarkets, farmers' markets, and Mexican grocery stores. Wines that pair well with tomatillos, cilantro, and lime are Albariño, Verdejo, and Riesling.

Pour 1 inch [2.5 cm] of water into a medium saucepan. Add the tomatillos, onion, jalapeño, and garlic and bring to a boil over high heat. Lower the heat to medium-low and simmer until the vegetables are slightly soft, about 5 minutes. Strain out the solids and reserve the cooking liquid. Set everything aside and let cool.

Transfer the vegetables to a blender and blend until smooth. Add a bit of the reserved liquid to thin out the sauce to your desired consistency. Add the cilantro and lime juice, season with salt and pepper, and blend again. Taste and adjust the seasoning, if necessary. Serve chilled or at room temperature.

MAKE AHEAD: The sauce will keep, tightly covered in the refrigerator, for up to 3 days before serving.

NOTE: If you prefer a hotter salsa, do not seed the jalapeño pepper. Be sure to wash your hands thoroughly after handling the pepper.

COCKTAIL SAUCE

MAKES ABOUT 1 CUP [225 G]

½ cup [130 g] ketchup

½ cup [130 g] store-bought
cocktail sauce

3 Tbsp horseradish

2 Tbsp fresh lemon juice

Dash of Worcestershire
sauce

Dash of hot sauce

Cocktail sauce is great to spoon onto raw oysters and clams, and it is *the* sauce to serve with classic shrimp cocktail. It's a snap to make with ingredients that are probably always in your refrigerator. Brut rosé and Pinot Gris complement the high notes of lemon and tomato.

In a medium bowl, combine the ketchup, cocktail sauce, horseradish, lemon juice, Worcestershire sauce, and hot sauce. Serve chilled.

MAKE AHEAD: The sauce will keep, tightly covered in the refrigerator, for up to 3 days.

MARINARA

MAKES ABOUT 3½ CUPS [790 G]

2 Tbsp extra-virgin olive oil

2 garlic cloves, minced

One 28 oz [794 g] can organic peeled and crushed tomatoes

1 tsp sugar

Pinch of red pepper flakes

Kosher salt and freshly ground black pepper

¼ cup [10 g] chopped fresh basil

Here is an all-purpose tomato sauce that is easy to prepare. It freezes well and is good to have on hand for a number of dishes. In addition to topping pasta and pizza, it makes an excellent dipping sauce for cocktail snacks, such as meatballs (pages 143–45) and *bocconcini* (Italian for "little bites"). Big tomatoey flavors are great with Sangiovese grape-based wines like Chianti Classico and Montalcino.

In a large skillet over medium-low heat, heat the olive oil. Add the garlic and cook, stirring frequently, until golden brown, about 2 minutes. Add the tomatoes, sugar, and red pepper flakes and season with salt and pepper.

Increase the heat to medium and bring to a simmer, then lower the heat to low and simmer, uncovered, for 30 minutes, stirring occasionally. Add the basil and stir. Cook for 5 minutes more. Taste and adjust the seasoning, if necessary. Serve warm.

MAKE AHEAD: The sauce will keep, tightly covered in the refrigerator, for up to 1 week and in the freezer up to 1 month.

TZATZIKI

1½ cups [360 g] Greek
   yogurt

1 small cucumber, peeled
   and finely chopped

2 Tbsp finely chopped
   fresh dill

1 Tbsp finely chopped fresh
   mint leaves

1 Tbsp extra-virgin olive oil

1 Tbsp fresh lemon juice

1 tsp lemon zest

Kosher salt and freshly
   ground black pepper

Tzatziki is a wonderful, refreshing yogurt-based Greek condiment that is usually served with grilled meat, fish, and poultry. It is especially good to eat with Lamb Meatballs (page 145) and Whole Poached Salmon (page 129). Try it with Pinot Grigio or Chenin Blanc.

Place the yogurt in a medium bowl. Add the cucumber, dill, mint, olive oil, lemon juice, and lemon zest and stir well to combine. Season with salt and pepper. Cover and refrigerate for at least 2 hours before serving. Serve chilled.

MAKE AHEAD: The sauce will keep, tightly covered in the refrigerator, for up to 3 days. Stir well before serving.

TRUFFLE CRÈME FRAÎCHE

MAKES ABOUT 1³/4 CUPS [400 G]

1 cup [240 g] crème fraîche

²/3 cup [160 g] mayonnaise

1 Tbsp truffle oil

Kosher salt and freshly
ground black pepper

Minced fresh chives, for
garnish

Here is a simple yet utterly indulgent and delicious way to doll up crème fraîche. Serve it as a luxurious dip with potato chips, crackers, or vegetables, or spoon a dollop of it over smoked salmon toasts. Nothing beats Champagne with this dip, but a dry rosé also makes a dreamy pairing.

In a medium bowl, mix together the crème fraîche, mayonnaise, and truffle oil. Season with salt and pepper. Garnish with chives and serve.

MAKE AHEAD: The crème fraîche will keep, tightly covered in the refrigerator, for up to 3 days.

ZUCCHINI CAPONATA

MAKES ABOUT 3 CUPS [640 G]

3 Tbsp extra-virgin olive oil

3 medium zucchini, trimmed and cut into ½ in [12 mm] pieces

1 red onion, chopped

1 cup [120 g] chopped celery

One 28 oz [794 g] can plum tomatoes with their juices, coarsely chopped

½ cup [70 g] kalamata olives, pitted and chopped

1 Tbsp balsamic vinegar

1 Tbsp drained capers

1 tsp sugar

Freshly ground black pepper

Caponata is most often made with eggplant; here's a flavorful version that is prepared with slow-cooked zucchini. It's good to serve as a dip with crispy pita bread or as a condiment with chicken, lamb, or steak. Merlot tastes great alongside it, as it's a wine that matches well with a wide variety of foods.

In a large skillet, heat 2 tablespoons of the oil over medium heat. Add the zucchini and cook, stirring occasionally, until golden, about 10 minutes. Remove the zucchini with a slotted spoon and set aside.

Add the remaining 1 tablespoon of oil to the pan and lower the heat to medium-low. Add the onion and cook until softened, about 3 minutes. Add the celery and cook until tender, about 10 minutes. Add the tomatoes and their juices and cook, stirring occasionally, for 10 minutes. Add the cooked zucchini, olives, vinegar, capers, and sugar. Season with pepper and simmer over low heat, stirring occasionally, for 10 minutes. Taste and adjust the seasoning, if necessary.

Serve at once or refrigerate (see Make Ahead) and serve warm, cold, or at room temperature.

MAKE AHEAD: The caponata will keep, tightly covered in the refrigerator, for up to 5 days.

CHERRY TOMATO CHUTNEY

MAKES 1 CUP [325 G]

1 lb [455 g] ripe cherry tomatoes, stemmed and halved

½ medium red onion, finely chopped

2 garlic cloves, minced

½ cup [120 ml] white wine vinegar

2 Tbsp granulated sugar

2 Tbsp brown sugar

½ tsp paprika

Pinch of dried thyme

Pinch of cayenne pepper or red pepper flakes (optional)

Kosher salt and freshly ground black pepper

You know that golden time of summer when you have too many cherry tomatoes and don't know what to do with them? There's a recipe for that: slow-simmered chutney made with ripe cherry tomatoes, a bit of sugar, vinegar, and spices. It's a wonderful condiment to serve with bruschetta, toasts, and grilled dishes, and you can prepare it in under an hour. If you like it spicy, add a pinch of cayenne pepper or red pepper flakes. Chilled light reds such as Pinot Noir or Cabernet Franc or a white Pinot Blanc are great choices for drinking with this summery sauce.

Combine the tomatoes, onion, garlic, vinegar, granulated and brown sugars, paprika, thyme, and cayenne (if using) in a medium saucepan. Bring to a boil over medium heat. Lower the heat to medium-low, season with salt and pepper, and simmer, stirring occasionally, for 35 to 40 minutes, or until the mixture thickens and is the consistency of jam or marmalade. Remove from the heat and let cool to room temperature.

Transfer to a clean container or jar and cover tightly. Serve at room temperature.

MAKE AHEAD: The chutney will keep, tightly covered in the refrigerator, for up to 3 weeks. Bring to room temperature before serving.

CARAMELIZED ONION & BACON JAM

MAKES 1½ TO 2 CUPS [490 TO 650G]

12 oz [340 g] slab bacon, diced

4 white onions, thinly sliced

¼ cup [60 ml] balsamic vinegar

2½ Tbsp brown sugar

1½ tsp mustard seeds

Kosher salt and freshly ground black pepper

This jam is fantastic to serve as a topping for bruschetta. When making it, it's important to give the onions plenty of time to caramelize over very low heat to let their natural sweetness shine through. What wine doesn't go with the porky, salty magic of bacon? My favorites are rich whites like Riesling and Pinot Blanc. Also, food-friendly Lambrusco is a great red choice.

Heat a large heavy saucepan over medium heat. Add the bacon and cook, stirring occasionally, until the fat is completely rendered and the bacon begins to crisp, about 12 minutes.

Drain off all but I tablespoon of the fat from the pan and add the onions, vinegar, brown sugar, mustard seeds, and I tablespoon of water and stir to combine. Cover the pan, lower the heat to very low, and cook for 15 minutes.

Remove the lid, stir again, and partially cover the pan. Cook until most of the liquid has evaporated and the onions have darkened and thickened, about I hour. Add a bit more water, if necessary, as the jam cooks. Season with salt and pepper.

Remove the jam from the heat and let cool slightly. Spoon into a jar or bowl and let cool completely. Serve warm or at room temperature.

MAKE AHEAD: The jam will keep, tightly covered in the refrigerator, for up to I week.

PLUM & GINGER JAM

MAKES ABOUT 1 CUP [325 G]

¼ cup [50 g] granulated
    sugar

¼ cup [50 g] light brown
    sugar

1½ lb [680 g] (about 12)
    ripe red or purple plums,
    halved and pitted

1 in [2.5 cm] piece fresh
    ginger, peeled and grated

1 red chile pepper, finely
    chopped, or ¼ tsp red
    pepper flakes

½ tsp vanilla extract

Ripe plums and fresh ginger are a fabulous flavor combination, and this jam is particularly good along with some sharp Cheddar cheese and a glass of dry red Malbec or port.

Pour 1 cup [240 ml] of water into a heavy-bottomed saucepan. Add the granulated and brown sugars and bring to a boil over medium-high heat. Lower the heat to medium-low and simmer, stirring, until the sugar is dissolved.

Add the plums, ginger, chile, and vanilla and bring back to a boil over medium-high heat. Lower the heat to medium-low and simmer, stirring occasionally, for 35 to 40 minutes, or until the mixture thickens and is the consistency of jam or marmalade. Remove from the heat and let cool to room temperature.

Transfer the jam to a clean container or jar and cover tightly. Serve at room temperature.

MAKE AHEAD: The jam will keep, tightly covered in the refrigerator, for up to 3 weeks. Bring to room temperature before serving.

FRESH FIG & ORANGE JAM

MAKES 1 CUP [325 G]

2 lb [910 g] green or purple figs, stemmed and cut into ½ in [12 mm] pieces

1 cup [200 g] sugar

½ cup [120 ml] fresh orange juice

Zest of 1 orange

Here is a great blend of flavors—fresh figs and oranges—that make a simple and mouthwatering jam. This is a very good accompaniment to cheese and charcuterie boards (see pages 66 and 148); pour Champagne or a sparkling white or rosé.

In a large nonreactive saucepan, toss the figs and sugar together and let stand, stirring occasionally, for about 15 minutes, until the sugar dissolves and the figs are juicy.

Add the orange juice, orange zest, and ½ cup [120 ml] of water and bring to a boil over medium-high heat, stirring until the sugar is completely dissolved. Lower the heat to medium and simmer, stirring occasionally, until the figs soften and the mixture thickens, about 20 minutes. Remove from the heat and let cool to room temperature.

Transfer the jam to a clean container or jar and cover tightly. Serve at room temperature.

MAKE AHEAD: The jam will keep, tightly covered in the refrigerator, for up to 3 weeks. Bring to room temperature before serving.

CHAPTER 9

WINE COCKTAILS

The following recipes for light, tasty, and inventive cocktails and aperitifs are made with wine. They are easy to make as single drinks or in batches, and they add a festive note to any event you might be hosting.

CHAMPAGNE POM FIZZ

MAKES 1 DRINK

1 oz [30 ml] pomegranate juice

4 oz [120 ml] Champagne

1 oz [30 ml] St-Germain Elderflower Liqueur

Splash of sparkling water or club soda

1 Tbsp pomegranate seeds, for garnish

Is there any drink more festive than a sparkling drink made with Champagne? Whether you're toasting a birthday, capping off an anniversary, or celebrating the holidays, this cocktail is always a winner.

Pour the pomegranate juice into a Champagne flute or coupe. Add the Champagne, liqueur, and sparkling water. Stir gently to combine. Garnish with pomegranate seeds and serve.

NOTE: If you're making a batch of drinks with Champagne, Prosecco, or Cava, a good rule of thumb is that two 750 ml bottles will make 10 drinks, four bottles will make 20, and so on.

KIR ROYALE

MAKES 1 DRINK

1 oz [30 ml] crème de cassis

4 oz [120 ml] Champagne

1 lemon twist, for garnish

Crème de cassis is a black currant-flavored liqueur that is produced in Burgundy, France. It is an essential ingredient in a kir (made with white wine) or kir royale (made with Champagne).

Pour the crème de cassis into a Champagne flute and add Champagne to fill. Stir gently to combine. Garnish with the lemon twist and serve.

AUTUMN BELLINI

MAKES 1 DRINK

1 oz [30 ml] unsweetened pear juice

1 oz [30 ml] pear brandy

4 oz [120 ml] Prosecco

1 thin pear slice, for garnish

The classic Bellini is made with Prosecco and a purée of white peaches. Here is a lovely seasonal twist on this traditional cocktail that uses pear juice and pear brandy. It's quite delicious.

Pour the pear juice and brandy into a Champagne flute and add Prosecco to fill. Stir gently to combine. Garnish with the pear slice and serve.

COCCHI SPRITZ

MAKES 1 DRINK

Ice

4 oz [120 ml] Prosecco

2 oz [60 ml] Cocchi
Americano

Splash of sparkling water or
club soda

1 orange wheel, for garnish

Fresh mint sprigs, for
garnish

A spritz is simply a drink that is prepared with sparkling wine, a splash of sparkling water or club soda, and often a dash of a bitter liqueur. Cocchi Americano is an Italian white wine *aperitivo* that is becoming more well known in the United States. It has a rather bitter flavor with citrus notes, and it pairs well with Prosecco to make this delightful drink.

Fill a wine goblet or rocks glass with ice and pour in the Prosecco. Add the Cocchi Americano and top it off with sparkling water. Stir gently to combine. Garnish with the orange wheel and mint and serve.

PROSECCO & GINGER SPRITZ

MAKES 1 DRINK

Ice

1 thin slice fresh ginger,
peeled

4 oz [120 ml] Prosecco

Splash of ginger beer

1 lime wheel, for garnish

Fresh ginger and ginger beer mixed with Prosecco makes a nice, bubbly, not-too-sweet cocktail that's perfect for summertime drinking.

Fill a rocks glass with ice and place the ginger slice in the glass. Add the Prosecco and top it off with ginger beer. Stir gently to combine. Garnish with the lime wheel and serve.

APEROL & CAVA SPRITZ

MAKES 1 DRINK

Ice

3 oz [90 ml] Cava

1½ oz [45 ml] Aperol

Splash of sparkling water or
club soda

1 large orange peel, for
garnish

Aperol is a classic aperitivo that originated in Padua, Italy, in 1919. It is made from a secret recipe of infusions that include sweet and bitter oranges, rhubarb, and a mix of herbs and roots. The Aperol Spritz has become very popular in the last few years with good reason—it's light, refreshing, and very tasty. Although it is often made with Prosecco, it is excellent with Cava.

Fill a wine goblet or highball glass one-fourth full with ice. Add the Cava, Aperol, and sparkling water. Stir gently to combine. Garnish with the orange peel and serve.

CAMPARI & RIESLING COCKTAIL

MAKES 1 DRINK

2 oz [60 ml] Campari

2 oz [60 ml] dry Riesling

Splash of sparkling water or club soda

Ice

1 lemon twist, for garnish

The bitter and sweet flavors of Campari and dry Riesling combine to make a wonderfully tasty drink. There are a number of good domestic dry Rieslings produced in Washington State and the Finger Lakes region of New York that would work wonderfully in this cocktail.

Pour the Campari, Riesling, and sparkling water into a mixing glass and stir well. Pour into a wine goblet filled with ice. Garnish with the lemon twist and serve.

WHITE WINE, ORANGE & MINT SANGRIA

SERVES 6

SIMPLE SYRUP:

¼ cup [50 g] sugar

12 fresh mint leaves

1 orange peel, cut into 3 in [7.5 cm] strips

COCKTAIL:

One 750 ml bottle Pinot Grigio, chilled

2 oz [60 ml] Grand Marnier

2 oz [60 ml] fresh orange juice

8 oz [240 ml] sparkling water or club soda

Ice

6 thin orange slices, for garnish

Dry Pinot Grigio complements citrus very well in this easy recipe. You may want to double the amount of simple syrup and keep the extra on hand in the refrigerator—it's a nice addition to cocktails, iced tea, and lemonade.

To make the simple syrup: In a small saucepan over medium heat, combine the sugar and ¼ cup [60 ml] of water and bring to a boil, stirring to dissolve the sugar. Remove from the heat. Add 6 of the mint leaves and the orange strips to the syrup. Let cool to room temperature, stirring occasionally. Strain the syrup, discarding the solids, and transfer the syrup to a large pitcher.

To make the cocktail: Add the Pinot Grigio, Grand Marnier, and orange juice to the pitcher and stir gently until mixed. Cover and refrigerate for 4 hours or until ready to serve.

Before serving, top off the sangria with the sparkling water. Pour over ice in tall glasses, garnish each drink with an orange slice and the remaining mint leaves, and serve.

ROSÉ & PEACH SANGRIA

SERVES 6

One 750 ml bottle rosé
wine

4 oz [120 ml] St-Germain
Elderflower Liqueur

2 oz [60 ml] brandy

2 ripe but firm peaches,
thinly sliced

½ cup [60 g] fresh
strawberries, hulled and
halved

8 oz [240 ml] sparkling
water or club soda

Ice

This light and beautiful sangria made with rosé, fresh peaches, and fresh strawberries is perfect to serve at summer picnics and barbecues. It's not too sweet and is very food-friendly.

Place the wine, liqueur, brandy, peaches, and strawberries in a large pitcher. Stir gently until mixed. Cover and refrigerate for 4 hours or until ready to serve.

Before serving, top off the sangria with the sparkling water. Pour over ice in tall glasses and serve.

ACKNOWLEDGMENTS

My thanks and gratitude to the people at Chronicle Books; to Tyrell Mahoney and Sarah Billingsley for seeing what this book could be and for making it happen; to Cristina Garces and Magnolia Molcan for their solid editorial support and for seeing the book through to the end with extraordinary care; to Design Director Vanessa Dina for her excellent design vision and her always-on-the-money advice; and to Tera Killip and Steve Kim for their production expertise.

A huge thank you to the wonderful Jennifer May for her incredibly beautiful photographs, and many thanks to food stylist Cyd Raftus McDowell and her assistant Cindi Gasparre. They all are the best in the business and working with them is always a pleasure.

Finally, a heartfelt toast and cheers to my many friends who know how to eat, drink, and celebrate in style and to my fabulous family, Lester, Zan, and Isabelle, who are always there for me.

INDEX